Tilting Toward the Sun

Tilting Toward the Sun

Love In the Balance

Mario Dell'Olio

While every precaution has been taken in the preparation of this book, the publisher assumes no responsibility for errors or omissions, or for damages resulting from the use of the information contained herein.

Tilting Toward the Sun
June 1, 2024.
Copyright © 2024 Mario Dell'Olio
All rights reserved. No part of this publication may be reproduced, restored in a retrieval system, or transmitted in any form or by any means, electronic, mechanical, photocopying, recording or otherwise, without the prior written permission of the author.

ISBN: 978-1-7330750-2-2

This is a work of fiction. Names, characters, businesses, places, events, and incidents are either the products of the author's imagination or used in a fictitious manner. Any resemblance to actual persons, living or dead, or actual events is purely coincidental.

To my immenso amore, my great love, Jim. Through tumult and delight, I can't imagine anyone else accompanying me on life's journey. Here's to forty more years together!

*For Dan and Steve, with whom we have wandered this path, our stories are intertwined. I am grateful that you remain a significant part of our
chosen family.*

*For Ted, Jeff, Michael, and countless others who we lost to AIDS—you have left an indelible mark on our hearts. Thank you for sharing your light
with us.*

PRAISE FOR

TILTING TOWARD THE SUN
LOVE IN THE BALANCE

"In this gripping novel, we see both the best of the human experience and the worst, reason for joy amid cause for despair, as we follow a romance from its burgeoning first days into a connection forged across tumult and triumph. A vital chapter in the American past and the tapestry of human love."
–Dr. Matthew Speiser, author of Sons of Liberty

"Fiercely powerful, Dr. Dell'Olio captains a harrowing and heroic journey through the AIDS crisis. Gaslit and victimized, Michael and Scott pursue a forbidden romance, risking their livelihoods and their lives. Tilting Toward the Sun is compulsively readable, inspiring, and hopeful, a fortress of courage and a memorial of love."
–Halo Scot, author of Edge of the Breach Series

"In Tilting Toward the Sun, Mario Dell'Olio once again proves he can write a love story to melt your heart."
–Claudia N. Oltean, Journalist, author of Another Chance to Die

"Mario Dell'Olio returns to the last century with a microcosmic view of the AIDS crisis, filled with heartbreak and solace, through the eyes of his beautifully-drawn characters. The author imbues his work with compelling historical context. This is an important book."
–Joanne Paulson, author of Blood and Dust, Adams Witness

"Tilting Towards the Sun is fiction wrapped around fact—of a bleak time in recent history. Accessible, enjoyable, entertaining, and emotional. It will pull at your heartstrings and make you want to scream in anger and frustration. Let's hope we never have to go through anything as horrific as this again."
–Terry Geo, Author, Playwright, Performer

"A heartwarming romance with carefully written prose and passionate dialogue by this brilliant author. This touching novel will transport you on a solemn voyage through the darkness, eternal brightness, and the unwavering hope of everlasting love. I heartily urge everyone to read this book!"
–Lali A. Love, author of The De-Coding of Jo Series

ACKNOWLEDGMENTS

Tilting Toward the Sun was born of my reflections on a generation of gay people who suffered through the AIDS crisis—some perished, others survived. These pages contain the stories of myriad people who sought only to love or feel a sense of belonging. Decades have passed since then and rarely have I thought of those dark days of loss. The intensity of discovering oneself, coming out, and searching for love was overshadowed by the fear of a disease that no one understood. We stood vigil, witnessing countless loved ones fall victim to a mysterious virus as politicians and religious leaders demonized our community. We feared for our lives, not only from AIDS but because of the hatred flung toward us through ignorance and prejudice.

Those of us who survived were marked by unimaginable loss. Some of us found love despite or because of our struggles. Survivor's guilt transformed into a solemn celebration of life. Finding love amid such devastation remains a miracle of unfathomable depth. For this, I am foreverthankful.

To Conor Bredin, you gave me a younger generation's perspective, navigating our history with a fresh mindset. Your sensitivity and support helped me dive deeper into my characters' hearts and minds. You challenged me to wade deeper into the conflict and pain of the period.

To Eileen Pollack, Joanne Paulson, Halo Scot: once again, your editorial prowess and expertise helped me to see what my eyes could not. You helped refine my manuscript with your keen talent for writing.

To my dear friend, Dr. Matthew Speiser: Words do not suffice in expressing my gratitude for your influence on my writing journey.

All at once, you prompt me to develop characters and scenes, include more historical context, while bolstering my confidence. I am inspired by your creative facility in your own writing, and I hope I have gleaned a bit of wisdom from your immense talent.

To my Twitter/X family, whose continued support for one another raises an entire generation of authors, especially The Writing Community Chat Show and my QueerIndie family. Thank you to Halo Scot, Christopher Aggett, Conor Bredin, Claudia Oltean, Lali A. Love, and the inimitable Steve O'Farrel.

A final note of thanks to my husband, Jim Alexander, for his continual support and love. Together, we have navigated dangerous waters, climbed the steepest mountains, and lifted each other up for nearly forty years. I can't imagine my life without you.

*"Years and years I have loved you
And dar'd not speak my love,
Your face was a light to lead my feet
To the crown of the Heav'ns above;
Lean closer, kiss me again, again,
For this is the Heav'n of Love."
—Gabriel Gillett 1863-1948*

CHAPTER ONE
FIRST GLANCE
Spring 1983

Scott needed to blow off steam. His rigid schedule at Johns Hopkins University had him wound more tightly than usual.

He had graduated at the top of his class at the U.S. Naval Academy and was one of the few allowed to apply directly to medical school. The typical path for newly graduated midshipmen was to serve five years in some capacity. After that service was completed, they could then consider further studies in fields useful to the Navy. Scott dreamed of becoming a doctor, but coming from a military family, his future was all but sealed. His brothers had joined the army, and Scott assumed he would do the same. When his appointment to Annapolis came, Scott was beyond thrilled. The Colonel loomed large in his life, and although his father served in the Army, Scott knew he couldn't be prouder of his youngest son. Scott glanced at the photo of himself and his father from commencement day. The two of them in formal uniforms were striking. Scott was proud of his accomplishments. Being in med school just a year later was a real coup.

However, life at the Naval Academy presented few occasions for him to be on his own. On the rare occasion he got away, he took full advantage of his freedom. Scott's life at Annapolis instilled the

importance of routine and following the rules. But he'd go insane if he didn't get out occasionally. Surrounded by fit, handsome men stretched his willpower to its limits and tested his strength. He trained himself to avert his eyes when classmates stripped down in the showers. There could be no hint of attraction at his prestigious military academy. So Scott kept his nose to the grindstone and buried himself in academics. When drinking with his buddies, he never let on he was gay. He played the game of the straight guy hot for the young women while at the bars—a part that every gay man was accustomed to playing in the early 1980s. Risky as it was, Scott needed to be with other gay men. Friendly and outgoing as an undergraduate at Annapolis, he was also known to be a loner. His classmates enjoyed ribbing him about going off on his own.

"You could have been a monk, Scott!" his bunkmate joked. "You can't get enough of your alone time."

"Yeah, what do you do on those solitary outings?" his buddy Mark asked. Do you meditate on the meaning of life?"

"Something like that," he replied with a mysterious grin.

Although he was no longer on the Annapolis campus, everyone at the university knew he was a naval officer. He had to maintain proper decorum at all times. There could be no question regarding his sexuality. But Scott was only human. He wasn't likely to be discovered as long as he traveled far from the university to seek social engagement.

Toweling himself off after a hot shower, Scott gazed at his reflection in the mirror. He liked what he saw—chiseled jawline, cut abs, and broad shoulders. He was in the best shape of his life. Surely, that would attract some attention at the bar. His tight jeans hugged his butt and accentuated his bulge in just the right places. He wore a plain white T-shirt, combed his jet-black hair, and spritzed himself with cologne.

Before long, he was in the gay neighborhood in Washington, D.C. As an undergraduate, Scott made regular pilgrimages to the bars whenever possible. Known for its art galleries and hippies, Dupont Circle attracted a vibrant young crowd, including political activists. The traffic circle boasted a park in the center that served as a gathering place and a location for political rallies. Bars dotted streets that led from the circle like spokes in a wheel. After parking his car, he strode to the

Lone Star, a high-energy bar featuring dancers in various undress stages. The atmosphere thrummed with excitement, making it a great place to engage with men in the audience.

As he approached the entrance, Scott scanned the block to see if he recognized anyone from Annapolis. It never hurt to be vigilant—he couldn't be seen at a gay bar. A dishonorable discharge from the Navy awaited anyone discovered to be gay. Not that there weren't gay people in the military—there were plenty among the ranks. They just had to remain deep in the closet. It wasn't uncommon for Scott to run into other guys from school, but they made sure not to interact back on campus, lest their classmates or faculty make assumptions. He realized getting involved with a fellow midshipman was far too risky.

Once inside, Scott shimmied up to the bar, ordered a beer, and made himself comfortable. A heavy sigh escaped his lips as he finally relaxed.

"Well, that was telling," the bartender said. "Must be a heavy load you're carrying."

"You have no idea," Scott replied.

"Oh, I think I do. Clean cut, fit body, Washington D. C. You're either military or government. Either way, you're hiding—deep undercover."

"Perceptive guy," was all Scott could say.

"Here, take this. It's on the house." The bartender poured a shot of whiskey and slid it across the bar.

Scott winked and thanked him as he turned to assess his prospects. It was such a relief not to avert his eyes and openly admire the cute guys gathered around him. The Lone Star was not an elegant bar. The cramped space had several high-top tables against the wall opposite the long wooden bar. One could walk across the room in fewer than ten paces when it was empty. But it was never empty on weekend nights. Scott could barely move without rubbing against another guy. Scanning the room, his eyes landed on the sweetest face. He had chocolate brown eyes and a mop of chestnut hair. Sweet Face's laugh was infectious and guileless. Then Scott noticed him chatting with a fair, classically handsome, and gregarious guy. Scott assumed it was his boyfriend since

they were very affectionate with each other. The blond turned his head toward Scott, and their eyes met. He locked in on his gaze like a guided missile and clawed through the crowd toward them.

"Hi there, I'm Scott."

"I'm Ted, and this is Michael," Ted said, motioning to the cutie who had first caught Scott's eye. "Quite a show tonight, eh?"

"Yup. It seems the dancers are getting more attention than usual," Scott replied as he tried to catch Michael's eye.

"Well, it doesn't hurt that the cowboy is hung like a horse," Ted said.

All three laughed, but Michael said little as Ted and Scott engaged in animated banter. Scott admired Ted's muscular arms and chest, a hint of washboard abs under his Izod polo, and piercing blue eyes. He was affable and handsome. It was easy to chat with him. But somehow, Scott was more taken with Michael. His light brown hair glistened under the lights like fairy dust, and when he looked up at the dancers, his deep brown eyes were a warm pool of desire. Scott enjoyed the comfortable conversation with Ted but knew it was only for show—totally superficial. While he couldn't be sure, he suspected Michael might be more substantial and was eager to chat with him.

"So, Michael, what do you do?"

"Ted and I are in grad school. You?"

"Same. What are you studying?" Scott hoped for more detail to get the conversation going.

"We're both in the counseling program at George Washington University. It's a great program." Ted said, jumping back in. "That's how we met; we've been inseparable ever since."

"Oh, are you boyfriends?"

Ted and Michael exchanged looks and laughed.

"Not a chance," Michael said. "Ted's too full of himself. Mr. I'm hot, and I know it."

"Hey, that's not fair. But I am hot!"

"Well, I can't argue with that," Scott said as his eyes scanned down to his tight package and back up, locking eyes with Ted. "But you're kind of adorable yourself, Michael."

"Such a sweet talker," Michael said, brushing off the compliment.

The three men spent the entire evening together. While they enjoyed their company, Scott hoped to get some time alone with Michael, but it wasn't in the cards.

"I'm beat, boys," Michael said around midnight. "I'm going to head out. Nice meeting you, Scott."

"Aw, come on, Michael. Stay for one more drink," Scott said.

"Are you kidding?" Ted interjected. "This guy can barely stay up past eleven. Can't you see? He's already turning into a pumpkin. See you back home, buddy."

"Have fun, boys. Try not to lead our new friend astray, Ted!"

Although he was disappointed, Scott and Ted made it to last call before exchanging numbers.

"I'd love to see you guys again, Ted. Let's be in touch."

Ted leaned in and gave Scott a warm, inviting kiss on the lips.

"I'll be sure to give your regards to Michael," he said with a wink.

•••

Driving back to Baltimore, Scott could think of nothing but Michael. He was deeply disappointed that he'd left so early. And while Ted was entertaining, there was no spark there. Besides, there was a lot of truth in Michael's estimation of him. He was full of himself and used any excuse to flex his biceps or pecs. He was obviously putting the moves on him, but Scott wasn't interested. The Naval Academy was full of fit guys strutting their stuff as if they were the cock of the walk. He hated that hyper-macho attitude and the military was full of it. Sweet and genuine guys were in short supply. He had to find a way to see them again. But how could he let Michael know he was interested without offending Ted?

CHAPTER TWO
NIGHT AT THE BAR
1983

     A week later, Michael lamented yet another night of drinking. It was the usual Saturday routine. Michael and Ted planned to go out around 10:00 p.m. Ted's favorite spot was the Lone Star because it had nude dancers, an electric crowd, and loads of congressional staffers looking for a bit of fun or a quick hookup. Michael preferred something quieter, but there weren't many options for a quiet gay bar in D.C. or anywhere, for that matter.

     Michael sang with a men's chorus, in which many members were gay. That was more his speed—meeting guys while doing something of mutual interest. He hated the bar scene—guys standing around staring down potential prey. It was always a cat-and-mouse game. You couldn't appear too interested lest you look desperate, but you had to give off some signal of interest, or you wouldn't get noticed—the art of the mating call. Michael couldn't stand it. Why can't guys just be themselves? Why does everyone have to appear unapproachable? he thought. At least the entertainment gave everyone something to talk about. If there was no one to chat with, you could watch the show. And what a show it was. The men danced on top of the bar, often interacting with the guys standing around. There was only one rule: Do not touch the dancers. It

was regularly ignored.

He and Ted chatted as best as they could over the thundering disco beat, always on the watch for cute guys. If things proceeded as usual, Ted would catch some stud's eye, and Michael would be abandoned for the evening. He had nothing against hooking up with some hot number—no moral qualms about it. Unfortunately, Ted seemed to garner all the attention when they went out. It happened so often that there appeared to be none left for him. Michael couldn't remember the last time someone cruised him. He knew he was attractive and fit, but he wasn't blond, he wasn't gregarious—he wasn't Ted.

As if his thoughts prompted reality, the scene played out right before him. An incredibly handsome man fought through the crowd and stood directly before them. Sure enough, he spent the rest of the evening chatting with Ted. This was getting old. Feeling like the third wheel, Michael headed to the bar. He hated being that close to the dancers—he never knew where to look when a performer writhed directly above him. If he looked up, he was staring right into his balls or butt. Michael just felt awkward. And on this night, it became more than uncomfortable. A particularly well-endowed fellow danced on the bar and spotted Michael as he looked away. Long Dong Danny was having none of that and stooped down as he shimmied his butt at the patrons behind him.

"Well, hello there, handsome. What fancy concoction do you have in that glass of yours? Let me see."

Michael, red in the face, held up his glass. Long Dong, who lived up to his name, took the drink from Michael and immediately dipped his ample appendage into the glass as if to sample the drink. Michael's eyes nearly popped out of his head. The crowd went wild with screams of laughter.

"Here you go, stud. That should make your drink a little sweeter," Long Dong said, handing the glass back to Michael.

So much for a quiet night out, Michael thought, staring blankly into his drink.

"Well, aren't you going to taste it?"

Michael was startled out of his catatonic state when he looked up to see Scott with the most adorable smirk on his face.

"Not on your life! Who knows where that thing has been?" Michael replied, scowling.

"Aw, come on, Michael. I'm sure Long Dong Danny is as pure as the driven snow."

"Yeah, snow after it's been trampled by an army of gay men," Michael replied as he put his drink on the bar.

"I'm sure that would simply add to the savory elixir you so desire."

"Perhaps you should finish it off, then."

"I'll pass," said Scott. "Where's your sidekick?"

"I think you've got that backward. The sidekick escaped to the bar after being abandoned once again."

"Is that so?" he said, leaning into Michael. "I just assumed the cuter guy had the sidekick."

"Oh, you are a charmer, aren't you? Is that why you never called Ted after our last encounter?"

"Ah, cute and perceptive. It seems my radar was spot on. How about I buy you a fresh drink?"

Much to Michael's surprise, Scott was sweet and interesting. He always assumed that hot men who exuded confidence were vapid and superficial. Or perhaps that was just his defense mechanism. If there were any justice, hot guys wouldn't be gifted with intelligence. It just wasn't fair to have looks and a brain. Scott proved him wrong, and the two chatted nonstop until last call. Time had flown by.

"One more?"

"Honestly, I really can't. I'm already sloshed. You might have to carry me out of here as it is," Michael slurred.

"That's an offer I'd happily accept. Let me walk you to your car?"

"I don't have one. We took the Metro."

"Then let me drive you home."

"That's pretty forward of you, Scott. Who said I was a bottom?" Michael quipped. The alcohol had loosened his inhibitions.

"Are you?" Scott raised his eyebrows suggestively.

"Wouldn't you like to find out?"

"Well, I was certainly hoping. Seriously, let me take you home,

Michael."

As soon as the car door slammed, they had their hands all over each other. Uncoordinated kisses led to clothes swiftly shed. Michael wasn't so drunk that he missed the muscular Adonis he held in his arms. When he found his way down below Scott's waist, he gasped at the turgid perfection that stood before him. Michael was voracious and driven by wanton lust as he engulfed Scott in his warm mouth. He couldn't get enough. When it was all over, they made eye contact and burst out laughing.

"So much for taking things slowly. I usually don't give it up on the first date."

"No worries," Michael replied. "I am, and you were incredible."

"Like I said earlier in the evening, you're definitely not a sidekick. You're the main event."

Back in his room, Michael could feel the dumb smile spread across his face. Ted hadn't come home and likely wouldn't be back until morning. He rarely cared, but Michael couldn't wait to fill him in on his evening with Scott. Ted had lusted after him the last time they were at the Lone Star. He wondered why he hadn't heard from him. Ted was not used to rejection. He just assumed Scott would call him. Michael loved Ted, but there was something delicious about the fact that Scott chose him instead of his buddy. *I finally got the guy, not Ted!* Michael sang.

He couldn't wait to see him again.

CHAPTER THREE
NOW WHAT?
1983

    The following morning, Scott could barely open his eyes. Although he hadn't been as drunk as Michael, he had overindulged. Scott knew driving back to Baltimore was a stupid move, but he was on autopilot, having driven the route so many times.

    He shuffled to the shower and let his mind wander back to the previous night. He couldn't have been more wrong about Michael. He wasn't shy in the least. Lathering himself up, Scott savored the image of Michael with a lustful and insatiable hunger. Scott was intoxicated by his assertiveness and sexual prowess. Images of their passionate encounter danced in his mind, leading to the inevitable. Scott let his soapy hands explore as he pictured Michael's crooked smile. The warm spray washing across his now lax muscles, his attention shifted, and he longed to see him again.

    It wasn't simply a lustful attraction. Scott was captivated by Michael's alluring openness. He only had to get him alone to read him like an open book. Michael was more than happy to share his family history and political views while he playfully made fun of himself. He ranted about how much he hated going out to bars, but there he was, every weekend, without fail. Michael chatted so much that Scott found it

easy to avoid telling him about being an officer in med school. He didn't know how to broach the topic but didn't want to chance any negative repercussions so soon in their relationship—if you could call it that.

But that was what he wanted. He fantasized about calling Michael his boyfriend, picking him up, and taking him out to dinner. As an officer, leading a normal life wasn't in the cards. Any future with Michael would be hidden from the public eye. They'd have to keep their relationship a secret. What kind of life would that be for Michael? He wondered if any gay men would agree to live in the shadows to be with a military man. Scott knew he was getting ahead of himself. Just let yourself enjoy getting to know him, he thought. You can figure out the rest when the time comes.

Buried in his books, Scott tried to concentrate on his studies, but to no avail. By noon, he stole away to his quarters and dialed Michael's number. Perhaps it was too soon, but he just needed to make contact—check in with him to see if what he imagined was real.

"Hello?" a groggy voice answered.

"Hello, Michael? This is Scott. Did I wake you?"

"Kind of. No. Yes. I don't know. I may have had too much to drink last night."

"What gives you that idea, handsome?"

"My pounding head and a mouth that tastes like an army marched through it."

"Or perhaps a navy?"

"What?"

"Nothing. Make sure you drink a lot of water and take a couple of aspirin. That will help with the dehydration."

"Good advice. Thanks, Scott."

"Anyway, I just wanted to say that I really enjoyed being with you last night. I hope we can do it again."

"Yeah, I did too. I still can't believe you wanted me instead of Ted," Michael admitted with a laugh.

"I told you last night his type doesn't interest me. Don't sell yourself short, Michael. You're a catch."

"I'm glad you think so. I'd love to see you again."

They made plans to meet for dinner the following weekend. Scott made reservations at Mr. Henry's, the casual gay burger joint on Capitol Hill. If he met someone from the military academy there, at least he could be confident they'd be friendly to other gay folks.

At long last, the day had come. He stood outside the restaurant, waiting for Michael to arrive and pacing anxiously. This is ridiculous, he thought. I should be excited, not nervous. Something about Michael made his breath catch. This one is special, he thought.

"Be careful there. You're going to wear out the sidewalk, fella," Michael called from behind.

"Where'd you come from? I just looked up that block."

"I must have rounded the corner at just the right moment. I'm not late, am I?"

"No, not at all. I was excited about seeing you—got here a little early," Scott admitted.

"Well, that's a lovely way to begin our date," Michael said as he leaned in and kissed him hello.

Scott's body went rigid. His fear of being seen took over. Scott was skittish and ducked into the restaurant. He was thankful they were seated quickly. Then, the server appeared and proceeded to hit on them. They giggled at his overt innuendos, and Scott's anxiety melted away. Before long, they fell into a flirty banter and soon chatted about old boyfriends and shared battle scars. Scott felt himself relax—spending time with Michael was so easy. He seemed completely comfortable in his own skin. He expressed his feelings openly, without fear of reprisal, and didn't play games. Scott couldn't believe it. On their first official date, he was already falling for the guy. Scott scooped up the check before Michael got a chance.

"This is on me. After all, I asked you out," Scott said.

"Fine, but I'll get the next one. Deal?"

"Deal! Meaning there'll be a next time?"

"Yes, unless you screw it up before the end of the night."

"Oh, that's a lot of pressure. I'm not sure I can be good for that long," Scott said and laughed. Hey, I'm not ready for the evening to end. Do you want to take a stroll to work off that tasty dessert?"

"My, that sounds perfectly civilized."

They wandered the neighborhood in contented silence. Then Michael stopped and looked at Scott.

"Sorry for being so self-centered—talking so much about myself. I still know little about you. You're studying medicine. Where? In D.C.?"

There it was—the conversation Scott was dreading. He resolved to be honest without revealing he was an officer.

"No, I'm studying at Johns Hopkins." Technically, Scott wasn't lying. The Navy was paying for his graduate studies in medicine.

"Oh, cool. That's a huge school; it's easy to get lost there. Do you like it?"

"Yes, it's great, but the first year of med school is insane. There's so much to get used to—lots of homework, late nights studying, and a ton of competition."

"Tell me about it. I can't wait to be in the workforce and get a regular paycheck. I'm tired of being a broke student," Michael said, seemingly satisfied with Scott's answer.

"Now that we know each other better," he said, raising his brow, "what do you say we head to your place? I assume Ted is at the Lone Star."

"You assume correctly." Michael's heart raced with anticipation. "I promise I won't be a sloppy drunk this time."

"Damn. That's too bad. I sort of liked that wild, sloppy Michael."

"Would you settle for a wild Michael who's not sloppy?" he said, grinning.

"Bring it on, handsome. Bring it on!"

Once in Michael's room, their playful banter morphed into passion. Without the urgency of the previous week's encounter, the two lovers explored each other's bodies, taking their time, savoring each touch, each taste. They were gentle and loving—passionate and lustful. Scott couldn't get enough of Michael's sensual lips and gently caressed them. Then he traced his finger along his jaw. Michael gazed at him with wonder in his eyes. Their bodies fit together like pieces to a puzzle, and they did what came naturally—without rushing. Dozing in each other's embrace, Scott couldn't believe how lucky he was to have found Michael.

He hoped this was a beginning for them. Knowing he had a long drive ahead, he rose from the bed reluctantly and dressed.

"Where are you going?" Michael asked. "Aren't you staying the night?"

"I wish I could. I have a busy schedule tomorrow," he lied. "Listen, I've loved every minute with you. I'll call you tomorrow."

Then he kissed him tenderly.

"Promise?"

"I promise. Now, go back to sleep and dream of me."

Driving back to Baltimore, Scott was consumed by desire. He wished he could stay overnight, but that was not allowed. His absence would be noticed. He loved being an officer in the Navy. It was his life—a life he had always dreamed of. Scott wished he could be an out gay man and do what he loved most. *Why is life so damned complicated?* he wondered.

CHAPTER FIVE
FREEDOM AT LAST
1980-1983

Michael's life back home in Virginia was quite ordinary. At least, that's what he thought. His family was squarely working class—his father worked in a factory, and his mom was a teacher's aide at an elementary school. Michael got along with his siblings, but they couldn't be more different. His brother, Hank, was the oldest and made sure Lisa and Michael knew he was top dog. Captain of the high school football team, his popularity trickled down to his sister and brother. It had certain benefits, for which Michael was grateful. No one bothered him about his lack of athletic prowess or penchant for the drama or the glee club. Most of his creative peers were teased mercilessly for being in such gay clubs. But Michael's sense of survival taught him how to pass as straight.

Living under Hank's shadow was challenging. Michael couldn't measure up to the big man on campus. There was no way he could compete with Hank. However, the girls who fawned over his brother included Michael in their affections.

"Your baby brother is so cute, Hank."

"Why aren't you as sweet as Michael? Come sit by us, baby brother."

Michael was grateful for the attention, which gave him instant status. He was adept at making conversation and learned to flirt in a non-threatening way. He was always surrounded by a swarm of young women, laughing and carrying on. Many older girls confided in Michael or used him to get close to Hank. Although Michael didn't date much in high school, no one even suspected he might be gay. Until he got to college, neither did Michael.

Roanoke College was Michael's obvious choice. His parents couldn't afford to pay for room and board, so commuting to school was a practical solution. It also allowed Michael to get a part-time job to help with the cost of books and his social expenses. He majored in social work and planned to pursue a graduate degree in counseling. Michael loved the program and the freedom that having a car provided. Although it wasn't glamorous, he got a job working at a McDonald's restaurant near the college campus. The guys worked at the grill in the kitchen—all but Michael. Since he could add quickly, they put him at the service counter. Pad and pencil in hand, Michael memorized the prices. He scribbled down the orders as quickly as possible, adding as he went along. Management doled out special pins as rewards for the quickest order takers. Those pins translated into raises, and every penny counted at $3.10 an hour.

Michael worked most weekend nights until closing. It was perfect for his schedule. By the time he helped clean up, the campus parties were in full swing. The best part of the closing shift was the leftover food. It was either dumped into the trash or given to the staff. Michael became a big hit, arriving at a keg party with bags of Big Macs or Quarter Pounders.

One night, just before closing, one of his classmates showed up at the counter. He and Derek often studied together in Derek's dorm room. Michael had a crush on him from the start. He was charming. Whenever Derek greeted Michael, he had a twinkle in his eye. Lying on Derek's bed studying, arms and legs often touched, and neither moved them apart as most straight guys would. Michael had never had sex with a girl or boy, so he wasn't sure how to respond to Derek's wrestling and tickling. All he knew was that he wanted more. When he showed up

right before closing, Michael perked up immediately.

"Dude, aren't you about done here?" Derek asked, knowing the answer.

"I'll be done soon. I can meet you at the party in twenty minutes."

"Forget the party. I'm sick of the same old crew getting drunk and puking all over the bathroom. My roommate went home for the weekend. Why don't we hang out in my room instead?"

"That sounds good to me," Michael said, intrigued by his invitation. Should I bring a few burgers?"

"I was hoping you'd offer. I have a craving for meat tonight," Derek said with a wink.

Michael didn't know what to make of his last comment but was titillated by Derek's flirty banter. When he arrived, Pink Floyd's "Dark Side of the Moon" set the mood in Derek's room. He had already taken a few drags from a joint and offered it to Michael. Although he didn't smoke often, he enjoyed the mellow feeling of marijuana. With a case of the munchies, they devoured the Quarter Pounders and the soggy fries. Leaning against the wall behind the bed, the two friends fell into their usual banter. Derek invariably found something to tease Michael about. He'd respond by playfully punching him in the shoulder, which inevitably led to wrestling. Both were high, and their wrestling ended with Derek pinning Michael to his bed. They laughed so hard that Derek collapsed on top of him. That's when Michael felt it against his thigh. *Does he have a boner? Holy Shit! He does, and so do I.*

Derek lifted his head—he smirked and pressed his hips against Michael.

"What do we have here? Is someone horny?" he said, leering at him. Then he lowered his face and slowly licked Michael's lips until he opened his mouth. Derek pressed his full lips against Michael's as their tongues probed with urgency. Moving to his side, Derek unzipped Michael's jeans and gripped his hardened sex. A groan escaped Michael's lips like a secret needing to be told. Before long, they were out of their clothes and exploring each other's warm, rigid bodies. No words were spoken while they satisfied their primal cravings.

"Dude, that was hot," Derek said when it was over.

"I... I've never done that before," Michael responded.

"Well, it certainly took you long enough. I've been trying to get a read on you for months."

"Honestly, I was afraid to be punched in the face and called a queer," Michael admitted.

"I get that, especially around here. Too bad we don't live in San Francisco or New York City."

"Maybe someday we will," Michael said. "So, does this mean we're boyfriends?"

"I don't know about that. But we can do this anytime you want," he said with a tickle.

Derek and Michael's relationship was not hot and heavy. There was no drama or deep romantic attachment. They were more like friends with benefits, which suited them just fine. Both Michael and Derek remained in the closet during their undergraduate years. Moving to Washington, D.C., for graduate school provided the perfect distance. Michael was too close to home to experience the freedom he truly desired. He hoped to blow the doors off his closet when he got to D.C. He was more than ready for a change.

•••

The university helped connect students in the same degree program. Ted was from Long Island, New York, and when they chatted on the phone, they hit it off immediately. It was dumb luck that his new roommate was gay, and Michael's crush on Ted was almost instantaneous. Finding housing for graduate school was challenging, but Ted and Michael discovered a place near Dupont Circle. Ted had that all-American athlete look—swimmer's body, perpetually tanned, with blond hair and blue eyes. He was not shy about strutting his stuff for anyone to admire, straight or gay. Walking around the apartment shirtless in only his Calvin Klein jeans and his physical displays of affection drove Michael to distraction. He was always hugging him or kissing him hello. Michael wasn't sure what to do with his feelings of unrequited desire. He hoped for romance. But Ted's open bragging about his sexual exploits made it clear they were only friends. Michael wanted more but resolved not to spend his energy on a hopeless cause. That didn't stop him from

fantasizing about hooking up with him someday. Whatever happened, Michael was thrilled that he was living in a proper city for the first time, and he was more than ready to take advantage of it.

Ted was out and proud on campus and was Michael's partner in crime for his newfound freedom. They immediately joined gay and lesbian organizations on campus and accompanied each other as they explored the gay bars of D.C. Michael was not a wallflower by any means—but compared to Ted, he seemed shy and reserved. Even though Ted slept his way through the membership in almost every club, people assumed they were a couple. They had an easy familiarity, and their affection was hard to miss. And while Michael basked in the joy of having a gay best friend for the first time in his life, he found it difficult to break free of his infatuation. Try as he might, there was rarely a strong connection with the guys he dated. None could compete with his feelings for Ted. Michael chided himself each time he found himself making the comparison. *You've got to stop this! Ted will never be your boyfriend.*

Michael wasn't sure if Ted was aware of his affections—he tried not to be too obvious lest he ruin their friendship. He didn't want to risk Ted distancing himself if those feelings were not mutual, and from what he could tell, Ted had other interests. He was constantly trying to fix Michael up with guys. They even went out on double dates. Michael knew he had to move on, and going to the bars with Ted was the perfect solution. Each time Ted hooked up with a new guy, Michael felt a bit of his infatuation wane. He loved him, but Ted was so self-absorbed that there was little room for Michael. Rather than get his feelings hurt, Michael found it amusing, laughing as each new conquest crashed and burned along with Ted's hangovers the following morning.

"So, Mr. Perfect wasn't so perfect after all?" Michael asked after watching yet another guy skulk out the door.

"Ugh! What a nightmare," Ted replied. "He wouldn't stop talking during sex. Honestly, I had to shove my dick in his mouth to make him shut up."

"That must have been pure torture. You poor thing."

"I know, right!? Why can't I find the right guy?"

"Perhaps it's because your quest for variety is insatiable?" Michael

added.

"Oh, yeah, that's probably it."

The two friends settled into a comfortable rhythm in their social lives and academic schedules. Months passed, and Michael's infatuation waned as their friendship deepened. Living in Washington with his new best friend opened up a new world for Michael. Although he didn't feel strong enough to come out to his friends and family back in Virginia, he developed a gay identity at the university. It was a significant step in accepting himself as a gay man.

CHAPTER SIX
EVADING THE SUBJECT
1983

Scott had enjoyed almost no free time while at the Naval Academy. Medical school was different; although the heavy academic program was very structured, his schedule was his own. The course load kept him in the library for hours every night, but his weekends were free. Washington, D.C., was just far enough away to provide anonymity and was the only place he felt comfortable being gay. And, of course, there was Michael. He was unlike anyone Scott had been with. He had a childlike sense of wonder and was a willing partner in any adventure Scott suggested. His easy affection and gentle manner were like heady drugs. When Michael reached out his hand to caress him, Scott turned to putty. He wasn't accustomed to guys holding his hand in public, let alone kissing him on the streets of D.C.

"What's wrong, Scott?"

"Nothing, why?"

"You got stiff as a board when I touched you—and not in a good way."

"No, I didn't. You just caught me off guard."

"Oh, sorry. So, now that you're ready, you won't mind if I just…"

Michael placed his hands on either side of Scott's head and kissed him right in front of the Smithsonian Museum. It happened suddenly, and Scott had no time to react. Heads turned, and Michael's mischievous grin met the eyes of passersby with steely resolve.

"Mikey, you're a crazy fucker. You know that? We're not in Dupont Circle. We could get beat up out here."

"Like anyone is going to mess with you—you'd knock 'em down with a single swing. And what have I said about calling me Mikey?"

"That's not the point, Michael. I just don't think we should invite trouble. I don't want to provoke anyone."

"Don't worry, my love, I'll protect you," Michael said, reaching up to pinch Scott's cheek.

"You're impossible. You know that?"

"I do. But that's what you love about me."

"Who said anything about love?" Scott teased. "I don't even know you."

The weeks turned into months, and Michael asked more questions about Scott's life. Scott had avoided specifics but knew he'd have to come clean soon. It was clear that he'd have to remain in the closet if he wanted to follow his career as a naval officer, but he couldn't imagine Michael giving up his freedom or putting up with hiding his affections. Scott was in too deep. He had fallen in love with Michael. *How can I risk losing him? I can't tell him—not yet*, he thought.

Michael wondered aloud why they never spent time at Scott's apartment and suggested hanging out with his friends. Whenever he brought up the topic, Scott changed the subject. But Michael continued to push, and he had to give a reason.

"I'm not out to most of them."

"You can't be serious, Scott. I can understand not being out to family back home, but you're in grad school, for God's sake."

"Granted." Scott needed to choose his words carefully, "But we each approach coming out in our own way. I'm sure you understand that from a counseling perspective."

"Point taken, but I know nothing about your life apart from your visits to D.C. I don't know, it just seems odd."

"Maybe my friends are boring. Or maybe I don't want to share you with anyone else."

"What a charmer. I was beginning to think you were ashamed of me."

"What? Are you kidding?" Scott said as he pulled him in for a playful hug. "I couldn't be prouder to have you by my side. You're beautiful."

Michael looked into Scott's eyes and drew his face closer—their lips touched, and he ran his tongue gently over Scott's. As Michael kissed him tenderly, Scott wondered how he got so lucky. But the conversations continued time after time. A few weeks later, Michael asked again.

"Why don't we stay at your place tonight? I'd love to get out of the city. Besides, we've been seeing each other for months, and I've never seen your apartment."

"I've told you I'm not out to my roommate, Michael. It will raise too many questions."

"Tell him I'm an old friend from high school. He won't suspect a thing. And I promise to be good!"

"You, be good?" Scott responded with a playful shoulder punch. "Fat chance. You'll call me honey and reach for my hand without a second thought."

"That's not fair. I can play butch and talk about sports. How about those Yankees?"

"The Yankees are a New York baseball team. They don't care about them in D.C. and Maryland."

"OK, whatever," Michael said, giving in. "At some point, you'll have to come out to him. You can't remain in the closet your whole life."

"Maybe, but this isn't the right time."

"Fine. When will it be, Scott?"

"I don't know," he said with a heavy sigh. "I honestly don't know."

Scott was grappling with coming out and his career. The two had always been mutually exclusive, and he was meticulous about keeping them in separate compartments of his psyche. He couldn't change his sexuality, and given his love for the military, he couldn't change his career. However, Scott couldn't bring himself to explain this to Michael.

"I'm sorry, Scott. I don't mean to push you on this. It's not fair to me. But I don't want to be your dirty little secret forever."

There it was. He'd said it—what Scott feared most. Michael would not tolerate living their lives together in the closet. And if he came out publicly, he'd be dishonorably discharged from the Navy. Scott's eyes filled with tears as he processed Michael's last statement. He pulled Michael into his chest and kissed the top of his head to cover his emotions. A single tear rolled down his cheek and into Michael's hair. What am I going to do? he thought.

CHAPTER SEVEN
A CERTAIN FUTURE
1970S

 Scott never questioned what the future held. A military career was all he ever wanted. Everything about it was attractive to him—the discipline, the order, the striving for perfection. Scott pushed himself to his physical and intellectual limits. His muscles strained while lifting weights—he felt exhilarated when jogging around the track. His most potent memories included watching young soldiers training on the base. He studied their bodies, each muscle extending and contracting in exertion and achievement. As a boy, he dreamed of becoming a soldier.

 Scott grew up feeling energized by competing with his classmates, especially his brothers. He and his older siblings were raised on military bases. Moving from one city and even one country to the next was commonplace. They had lived on bases in Germany, the Philippines, and Panama. They were used to making friends quickly but remained somewhat detached. Knowing they would move after two or three years, the brothers kept an emotional distance from new friends. Only a year apart from one another, Scott and his brothers were the best of friends and fervent enemies. The bond they formed as young boys was the only constant in their lives.

Adventures off base were legendary as they broke the rules and incurred their father's wrath. In Panama, the brothers explored the jungle and participated in scouting activities with the usual sense of invincibility and exhilaration of youth.

One of their favorite stories was when they nearly got arrested. A thick bamboo grove grew on government property right in Panama City. The boys figured the strong stalks would make the perfect material to build a log cabin and set about cutting down the largest canes they could find. The only requirement was portability. After a bountiful harvest, they dragged the canes down the city's main street back to the military base. They never made it home. Their father, the Colonel, received a call from the local police requesting his presence immediately.

With heads hanging, the three boys barely looked up when the police chief greeted the Colonel. In full uniform, he strode past his sons and into the chief's office. All they could hear through the closed door were murmurs. Sweat dripped down their temples as they awaited the imminent storm. Instead, the Colonel calmly strode out of the office and motioned for them to follow. His silence did not bode well for them. The short ride to the base was sheer torture. No one said a word. Once in the house, the Colonel motioned to the couch, and the boys sat.

"Do you have any idea what you've done? Of course, you don't because you don't think before you act."

"We're sorry, Dad…" Mitchel began.

"Did I say you could speak?"

All three heads snapped to attention. This was bad. Really bad.

"What possessed you to trespass on the governor's property? Not only did you trespass, but you cut down ancient bamboo in a protected grove. Then you dragged it down Main Street for everyone to see. What were you thinking? Our relationship with the government requires a delicate dance. You not only put me in an uncomfortable place but the United States Government as well. What possible reason could you have for doing what you did? Now, you may speak."

"We didn't know it was a protected grove," Mitchel said.

"It looked like any other bamboo forest, Dad, honest," Wayne added. "We just wanted to build a log cabin."

"That is not an excuse. You should know better," the Colonel said as he removed his belt.

They knew what was coming. It wouldn't take very long, but the sting on their bare bottoms would last for days. Scott remained silent with each snap of leather on his buttocks, whereas his brothers wailed in pain. He would never show weakness in front of his father or make excuses for poor decisions. His father instilled in him a respect for rules—breaking them came with consequences. Scott accepted his fate with respectful deference if he was caught. Although the bamboo incident, as it came to be known, seemed extreme, the three brothers did not curb their antics. They palled around, fought like enemies, and were each other's fiercest defenders.

Trips to the emergency room for broken arms, split lips, or stitches were common occurrences. Their poor mother gave no sympathy when they'd inevitably come crying to her after a fight.

"Serves you right—fighting like animals. Get in the car, and don't get blood on the carpet!"

That was family life for Scott—but he wouldn't change it for the world. The richness of his childhood experiences formed him into the man he had become. Living all over the world and making new friends with every move gave him the facility to engage people in conversation, no matter the circumstances. He often started conversations with store clerks or while standing in line at theaters. Scott could chat with anyone regardless of age or background and truly enjoyed meeting new people. It didn't hurt that he was handsome and had a winning smile.

Scott's success was not attributed to his looks and affability alone. He was naturally curious and drove his teachers to distraction with continual questions. His mother came home one day to find him sitting on the living room floor with her vacuum cleaner entirely dismantled. Each part was meticulously lined up in the order Scott had removed it.

"What have you done?" she screamed.

"I took it apart, Mom."

"But why? Do you know how much this will cost to repair?"

"I wanted to see how it worked. Don't worry; I can put it all back together. It'll be better than new," Scott said confidently.

True to his word, the vacuum cleaner worked better than before, and Scott was on to his next project. His intellectual curiosity never flagged. By the time he reached high school, he was known for his athletic prowess and sharp mind. His valedictory speech at commencement inspired and challenged his classmates to serve their country, look beyond their selfish gain, and work for the greater good. His appointment to the Naval Academy in Annapolis was no great surprise to his classmates. Scott was destined for greatness.

Driven as he was, Scott rarely addressed the elephant in the room. A gaggle of girls chased after him throughout high school, but he never dated much. His interest in other boys was buried so far beneath the surface that no one suspected he might be gay. Given Scott's career choice, keeping his sexuality a secret suited him perfectly. It was nobody's business but his own.

CHAPTER EIGHT
MILITARY WHITES
SUMMER 1983

Scott donned his freshly pressed military whites. The crease on each leg of his trousers was sharp as a razor's edge. His shoes shone so brightly he could see his reflection. The final touch was his hat—once placed upon his head, Scott presented an impressive figure. He gazed at himself in the mirror—broad shoulders and chest, square jaw, and the outline of his biceps bulging through his white suit coat. Nothing like a man in uniform, he said aloud and laughed. If only Michael could see me now. Maybe he'd be so enchanted with his navy man that he'd agree to anything. Scott shook his head and drove to Annapolis to pick up a few recent graduates and one of his classmates. Pulling up to the entrance, Scott saw they were already gathered.

"It's about time, Lieutenant. How long did it take to squeeze those bulging muscles into your whites?" his buddy Glen quipped.

"Right?!" Charlie joined in. "Or perhaps our Narcissus got lost in his reflection."

They pealed with laughter.

"All right, men," Scott responded. "Knock it off, or you'll be hoofing it on your own. Remember, I'm the one with the car."

"Yes, Sir!" they intoned in unison.

The four officers piled into Scott's car, and they headed north. Senator Sarbanes from Maryland loved meeting the newly minted officers from the Naval Academy. Since he'd served on the Judiciary and Ways and Means committees in Annapolis, his affection for the midshipmen and officers grew. Each summer, he hosted several Annapolis officers for lunch.

"This isn't your first time lunching with the senator, is it, Scott?"

"No, Sir. Although I didn't graduate this year like you kids, he clearly sees my unique leadership skills. I'm so charming. The senator just had to see me again."

"You're so full of shit," his buddy Glen responded.

"Wait. You guys are in the same class. Why didn't he invite you last year?" Charlie asked.

"Hey now, I was on leave."

"For the entire summer? I don't think so," said Charlie.

There was a brief pause in their joking. They were painfully aware that Glen was among Annapolis's few people of color. None of them wanted to believe he wasn't invited the previous year because he was Black. However, prejudice was always present, and Glen understood he had to play by different rules.

"Well, anyway. Where do you think we'll go?" Glen asked, redirecting the conversation.

"The senator usually takes the young officers to the Jockey Club. It's the place to see and be seen in D.C. Who knows? We may spot a few Hollywood stars amid the politicians."

"Seriously? That's so cool!"

Scott found parking on the street, and the four young officers climbed the Capitol stairs. After checking in, they strolled the long corridors to the senator's office. Scott had been there many times, but it always impressed him. This was the seat of their government, the legislature. It was a temple of democracy. After a brief delay in the waiting room, Senator Sarbanes invited them into his office. He slapped each on the back as if they were old friends, putting them at ease.

The senator's driver dropped them at the entrance of the Jockey

Club. Once inside, they were swept into the energetic crowd. It was a veritable who's who of D.C. powerbrokers. The senator schmoozed anyone who caught his eye and made sure he was photographed with the handsome young officers. The guys felt like celebrities, and Scott enjoyed every admiring glance he received, especially from some young staffers. The gay underground was alive and well in the Capitol, and Scott played the game expertly. The senator offered the young men a ride back when the meal was finished.

"Thank you so much, Senator, but we rarely get up to D.C.," Glen replied. "I think we'll take advantage of our freedom and walk around the city."

"Great idea, son," said Senator Sarbanes. "I'm sure you handsome fellows will catch a few admiring eyes. Those single ladies love a man in uniform."

They chuckled as they shook his hand, then wandered into the street. Just a few blocks away was Dupont Circle. Scott was apprehensive, not knowing how his buddies would react to being in a gay neighborhood. He hung back and let Glen take the lead.

"I love this part of town. There's always a lot going on and loads of bars to check out," Glen exclaimed.

"Lead the way, then. You can be our tour guide," Scott replied, reasonably sure he knew the neighborhood better than Glen.

The guys didn't seem to notice all the men hanging out together. As the young officers strolled by, heads turned. The senator was right about one thing, Scott thought. Admiring eyes are indeed fixed on us. But they are all gay men.

"Let's pop in here and grab a beer," Glen suggested.

Scott was relieved that it was not one of the overtly gay joints he'd hung out in, but he knew the bar would have a mixed crowd. After a few beers, they were feeling no pain. Their animated conversation and their white navy uniforms attracted a great deal of attention. When it was Scott's turn to buy a round, he strode to the bar and held out a twenty-dollar bill. The bartender came to him immediately.

"What can I get you, sailor?" he said with a mischievous grin.

"How can you tell?" he said, playing along. "Was it the haircut

or the stripes on my uniform?"

"Oh, are you wearing a uniform? Your rippling muscles are so imposing I didn't even notice."

"You're a charmer. Can I get four Buds, please?"

"Coming right up."

Filling the mugs from the tap, the bartender continued to flirt with Scott.

"We don't usually get your type in here, at least not in uniform. What brings you to our fine establishment?"

"We had lunch at the Jockey Club with our senator. The guys have no idea this is a gay bar. I'm just playing along."

"All right then, I won't ruin your cover." The bartender winked and said, "These are on the house. Come by again without your entourage."

"You're a prince. Thanks, man," Scott responded and winked back.

Glen noted their interaction and immediately pulled Scott aside. He was pretty buzzed as he tried to whisper in Scott's ear.

"Dude, I think the bartender is into you."

"You're crazy and drunk," Scott said, trying to deflect Glen's comment. "Here, finish your beer, and let's get out of here."

"I'm serious, Scott. I'm pretty sure this is a gay bar."

"Well, you picked it. But don't worry, no one's looking at you," Scott said, slapping him on the back.

"Fuck you! I bet I could pick up any guy here if I wanted."

"I bet you could. Then the Navy would kick your ass right to the curb," Scott said.

"No kidding. We should go, just in case any spies are around.

They joined their buddies and finished up their beers. Glen's comment made Scott wonder if he could be gay as well. He seemed awfully familiar with the neighborhood, too. Scott hoped to have at least one gay friend in the Navy. But he had to play it close to the vest. He couldn't risk being found out.

The once-crisp uniforms bore a few wrinkles as the officers stumbled out of the bar. They were boisterous and in good spirits as

they walked down Massachusetts Avenue. If Scott thought they were attracting attention after lunch, it was multiplied tenfold after all the alcohol they had consumed. The guys were clueless as their boisterous behavior focused every eye on them. He enjoyed the irony of his straight buddies being ogled by the gay men passing by. Then, a familiar voice startled him out of his buzz.

"Scott? Is that you?"

"Michael, hi," he stammered. "What are you doing here?"

"I live here, as you know. What's with the uniform?"

The guys finally noticed Michael and stopped walking. At face value, there was nothing particularly unusual about running into friends in D.C. But Glen picked up on the tension and zeroed in on their interaction.

"I, um, we had lunch with Senator Sarbanes from Maryland. Then we just stopped for a drink."

"From the looks of it, you've had quite a number of drinks," Michael said, showing his irritation.

"Hi, I'm Glen, and this is Charlie. This is Sam," Glen said, holding out his hand.

"Oh, hi, I'm Michael. Nice to meet you. I gather from your uniforms that you're all from Annapolis."

"Yeah, Scott and I graduated last year, and these guys are newbies. How about you?" Glen asked.

"I'm at GW, getting my master's in counseling."

Scott composed himself and jumped in.

"Michael and I are old friends. I forgot he lived in the neighborhood."

"Yes, we are the best of friends," Michael said through gritted teeth. "I wish I could stay and chat, but I need to get to class. It was great to meet you guys. See you later, Scott."

Scott didn't know what to do as they continued in the opposite direction. Michael's clipped responses and stiff gait told Scott all he needed to know. Michael left fumes in his wake as he walked away.

"Listen, guys. I just remembered that I had to tell Michael something. I'll catch up."

"No problem, Scott," Glen said. "We'll meet you at the car."

Thank God for Glen. Scott could tell he suspected something. He was covering for him. But why? Does he suspect something? Scott shook his head and sprinted to catch up with Michael. He had to explain.

"Michael, Michael, wait up!"

He turned rigidly and said nothing.

"Look, I'm sorry. I know I have a lot of explaining to do."

"You think? When were you going to tell me you're in the Navy?"

"I meant to tell you dozens of times. I just lost my courage. I know you're pissed, but let me explain. Can we get together tonight? I need you to understand."

"What's to understand? You've lied to me for months. What's so urgent now?"

"Please, Michael, just give me a chance."

"Fine. But I can't promise you anything. Let's meet at eight by the Lincoln Memorial. That'll give you time to sober up."

Without waiting for an answer, Michael turned and walked away. Scott's gaze never left him. *How could I have let this happen?*

CHAPTER NINE
IS IT OVER?
1983

Michael clenched his fists as Scott stood before him in his military whites. Damn him for looking so hot! He barely heard anything he said. He felt betrayed. Why had he lied to me for so many months? What was there to explain? Scott's pleading eyes bore into him, and he relented. At least he had a few hours to compose himself. Michael ran the scene over and over in his mind. He had so many questions. Was Scott embarrassed for himself or ashamed of being with Michael? What did this mean for their future? Was there a future for them? Could he ever trust Scott after his deception? Michael was reeling as he sat in class.

"Are you with us today, Michael?" the instructor asked.

"Sorry, professor. I'm a little distracted."

"Yes, everyone can see that."

When he got back to his apartment, he shed his clothes and jumped into the shower. The hot spray almost burned the back of his neck, but he remained there for nearly thirty minutes. Try as he might, he could not wash away the tension. He climbed out of the tub and toweled himself dry. Despite his anger, Scott's chiseled features danced in his mind. He struck an impressive figure in his uniform, and Michael

became aroused. Stop it! He just lied to you. Michael wiped the fog from the mirror and stared at his reflection. His eyes expressed what his heartfelt. The blow dryer made his hair fly in all directions—he needed a haircut. Even so, he marveled at how shiny it was and how auburn—highlights gave his chestnut hair depth. It was the attribute where his vanity showed. He couldn't remember when he'd felt this good about himself. Much of that was because of his relationship with Scott.

He threw on a pink Izod and his Calvin Klein jeans. His navy blue canvas belt had a bright pink stripe that matched his polo perfectly. Michael wanted to look especially good tonight. They planned to meet on Capitol Hill, away from the gay neighborhood and away from his apartment. Michael didn't want any distractions and didn't trust himself to be alone with Scott at his place. Resisting Scott's charm and magnetic allure was nearly impossible. He still had a few hours to kill before their date, and Michael was restless. He paced in his tiny room, checking his watch every so often.

Ugh! I need to get this over with. Waiting is driving me crazy.

•••

The drive back to Baltimore was torture. Scott could not stop thinking about the look on Michael's face. His eyes screamed betrayal. Scott wasn't sure what was worse—the fact that he'd hurt Michael or the fear of losing him. On top of that, Glen had been cagey after meeting Michael. He was suspicious, and Scott waited for him to bring it up. Luckily, Charlie and Sam were three sheets to the wind, telling tales of their latest conquests in the back seat. Scott and Glen walked them to their quarters when they got to campus. Glen hung back and pulled Scott aside.

"Hey Scott, you've been pretty quiet since we got into the car. Everything all right?"

"Yeah, sure. Trying to concentrate on driving. I probably shouldn't be behind the wheel after drinking so much."

"Nothing you haven't done before. It just seems like something else is bothering you," Glen pressed him. "Ever since we ran into your buddy, Michael, you've been on another planet."

"You're imagining things," Scott said. "What could be bothering

me?"

"I don't know. Why did you run after him, then? That was weird."

"Why? I just forgot to tell him something. Don't make a big deal about it."

"Hey, Scott, no need to get defensive. It just looked like you guys were upset about something. You could cut the tension with a knife."

"Nah, he was just surprised to see me in my uniform. You know how these liberals hate the military."

"You mean he didn't know you're an officer? Why wouldn't you have told him?"

"It's complicated."

"Complicated? Could you be any more evasive?"

"I don't know what you're getting at, Glen. It's hard to explain, that's all."

"Try me. Look, it's just us here. Sam and Charlie are gone. Tell me what's really going on."

"Nothing is going on!" Scott said, raising his voice. "Just let it go."

"Whatever. Just be careful, Scott."

"What do you mean? Why do I need to be careful?"

"Dude, we've been friends since our first day at Annapolis. Let's not play games. That guy means something to you."

"What are you implying, Glen? This is not funny."

"I'm not implying anything. I'm just saying that you can trust me—with anything."

Scott didn't like where the conversation was headed. He wasn't ready to take any risks with his military career—not when he was just starting medical school. Scott had always been a master at keeping an air of mystery around him. His image was the All-American Boy—athletic, intellectual, and patriotic—one he carefully cultivated throughout high school and at Annapolis. It was the standard to which all midshipmen strove at the Naval Academy. Scott's confidence beamed, and he approached every social situation with equanimity and charm. Glen's probing questions rocked his comfortable world. He had to redirect the conversation and take control.

"Just let this go. Michael is an old friend. That's all."

"So that's how it's going to be, Scott?"

"Look, buddy, I'm not sure what you're getting at, but I don't like it. You would do well to stay in your own lane here."

"Getting testy there, Scott. What's got you all hot under the collar? Could I be hitting too close to home?"

"Damn it, Glen! This is not a game." Scott raised his voice. "You, of all people, should know that the mere implication of impropriety could get me tossed out of the Navy."

"And who's going to report you, me? Come on! I'm your best friend. We have been through it all—together."

There was a moment of silence. Then Glen spoke.

"Scott, you're the only white dude I trust here. I am careful around everyone else but you. So, hear me when I say I know what being alone is like. I'm the only Black guy in our class. Don't you think I understand what it's like having to prove myself at every turn? I strive to be better than our classmates so I can be judged as equal. And even that isn't enough. I can't afford to fuck up. And you do the same thing, albeit for different reasons. But in this case, we're playing on the same team," Glen said, looking him straight in the eyes.

Scott looked around to see if anyone was close by. He thought he'd been so careful. If Glen could figure out his sexual orientation, so could the others. He wasn't sure how to respond. *Should I deny it, act as if he's out of his mind? On the other hand, it would be such a relief to have a gay friend in the Navy.*

"Earth to Scott," Glen said, snapping his fingers before his face. "Did you hear me?"

"Yeah, yes, sorry. I don't know what to say."

"Come on, Scott. Can't we be honest for once? I could use a friend, too."

Scott shook his head and sighed. Turning, he took a few paces, and Glen followed. Neither said anything as they continued to walk. So many thoughts rushed through Scott's mind. For the first time in years, he wasn't in complete control of his emotions. Perhaps it was because he had fallen in love. The scene with Michael had knocked him off

balance, and now Glen was pushing the envelope. He didn't know how to respond to Glen. His mind told him to keep his distance and deny it while his heart ached for a friend to confide in.

Glen and Scott had become fast friends from the very first day. Their friendly competition reminded him of his brothers. Who could do the most push-ups or run the quicker mile? There could never be a tie. One of them had to win. They pushed each other to their limits and celebrated their achievements. And their friendship was more than that. They could share their frustrations with classmates or teachers without fear. There was no false bravado with Glen. Whereas the rest of their classmates bragged about picking up chicks and reveled in sexual language, Glen never did. If the guys gave either of them a hard time about it, he would simply say, "My mother brought me up better than that." As he looked back on it, perhaps Glen was protecting the same secret. Scott looked straight ahead as they walked. He needed a friend right now.

"You're right, Glen. We've supported each other from the start. Without your friendship, Annapolis would have been a desert. And right now, I could use my friend."

"I'm right here, man. Talk to me."

"My entire life has centered on getting to where I am today. I love the Navy, and I love being in medical school."

"I know you do, and I get it. There's nothing I want more than my career as an officer. This is my life."

"So, why risk it?" Scott asked.

"Because neither of us can change who we are or who we love."

At that, Scott stopped walking and turned to his buddy. His eyes were wide with respect, or perhaps it was gratitude? Glen had just spoken what he could never articulate.

"There it is," he said. There was more silence, but the gap between them had closed. Then he spoke.

"Look, Glen. I trust you with my life. I've watched you navigate prejudice with calm composure. I have always admired you for that. But I know it comes at a cost. You hold a lot of emotion at bay. It's nowhere near the same thing, but I cringe at every fag joke or each time they call

us ladies. I'm just so uptight about this. I love the Navy and don't want anything to jeopardize my career."

"Well, don't worry, buddy. I have as much to lose as you. There's no reason to go through it alone."

Scott let out a heavy sigh. The weight he'd been carrying for years finally lifted from his shoulders.

"So, tell me, what's really going on with Michael?"

For the first time since he stepped foot on the Naval Academy campus, Scott spoke candidly about being gay and falling in love. Glen proved to be a good ear and shared his fears regarding their future in the military. Both had so much pent-up frustration and anxiety.

"I'm not sure what's going to happen now," Scott admitted.

"You guys will never get to be a normal couple. You know that, don't you?"

"That's the problem. I don't think Michael will stand for that. I mean, why would he?"

Sharing his fears and frustrations with Glen was like a balm to his wounded heart. They walked and talked for over an hour. He was almost late for his date with Michael. When he got home, he flew into his apartment and hopped into the shower. It was ridiculous that he had to turn right back around and drive to D.C. for the second time that day. But Michael was worth it. Scott had to fix this.

CHAPTER TEN
REFLECTING POOL
1983

They agreed to meet at the National Mall near the Lincoln Memorial. Michael loved the reflection pool. He hoped it would be a familiar place to wander as they sorted through this mess. He arrived nearly thirty minutes early, enough time to climb the steps to the memorial. No matter how often Michael had been there, it never failed to move him. The stark white statue of Lincoln was grand and imposing—it exuded strength and conviction. Even though gay folk continued to be marginalized and oppressed, he believed Lincoln stood for equality for all.

Michael had become increasingly active in seeking gay rights while in Washington. It was the perfect city for fighting for legislation and making his voice heard. He joined as many gay political organizations as his schedule allowed. There was always a lecture or a protest to attend. Michael felt as if he were making a difference. The impetus for becoming a counselor was to help young people who struggled with sexual orientation and identity. His activism dovetailed perfectly with his goal.

After visiting the memorial, Michael felt more centered. Now that his emotions had ebbed, he was ready to chat with Scott. He didn't

know what would come of their discussion, but he resolved to follow his heart. It had never led him astray before. He had made painful decisions in the past, and he trusted the voice inside. He scanned the base of the reflecting pool for Scott and spotted him. I do love him. We just have to work this out, he thought.

The crowd was sparse for a late summer evening at the mall. Michael made his way down the steps, and Scott turned and looked up. Michael waved, and Scott flashed a tentative smile. He really is adorable, Michael thought.

"Hey, I got here a little early, so I wandered around the monument," Michael offered, not knowing what to say.

"It's beautiful, isn't it?" Scott began. "Lincoln's words are so inspiring."

"It always makes me feel like anything is possible in this country—as if we can right any wrong or injustice."

"It's why I chose to be in the Navy—to serve this great country."

"To serve this country posing as a straight man."

Michael's jab was pointed and hit its mark.

"Those are the rules, Michael. If hiding is the only way I can serve, I am willing to make that sacrifice."

"But if the rules or laws are unjust, they should certainly be changed. Isn't that what Lincoln did when he signed the Emancipation Proclamation? If we don't speak up in the face of injustice, how can we live up to the ideals of this country?"

"Of course, you're right, Michael. But the real world doesn't work like that. Sometimes, we have to work with what we've got."

"And what we've got is a system that is oppressing gays and lesbians."

There was an awkward silence as their last encounter created a distance between them. The August humidity hung heavily as they strolled beside the pool. The Washington Monument was lit up, and its reflection danced as the warm breeze created ripples on the water's surface. A crescent moon shone brightly above them. If not for the tension, it would have been peaceful. Neither of them knew how to start. Finally, Scott reached out, putting his hand on Michael's shoulder.

"Let's walk."

After more silence, he spoke again.

"Michael, I'm so sorry I deceived you. I never meant for it to last this long. I know it's no excuse, but I didn't want to risk losing you."

"I suppose I understand that, but this is pretty big. I'm still trying to figure out what the repercussions are for us. You're an officer in the Navy."

"I am, and I'm in love with you."

Before that moment, they hadn't spoken those words. Michael stopped in his tracks and stared at him.

"In love with me?"

"Yes. I think about you all the time—when I should be studying or listening to a lecture, in the lab—all the time."

"But is that love, Scott? I don't know. Does one lie to someone they're in love with—for months?"

"Consider it a sin of omission,"—more silence—"I'm sorry. I never meant to keep it from you for so long. The longer I waited, the more difficult it became, and the more I feared losing you."

"So, what do we do now? I mean, what happens to us?"

"If you can forgive me, I want us to be together. Like I said, I love you, Michael."

"And I love you too. But how can this work? If we're discovered, you'll be thrown out of the navy. Won't they stop paying for medical school?"

"Yes. We'd have to be very careful. But I'm willing to try if you are. What do you say?"

"I don't know if I can, Scott. I worked so hard trying to accept myself. I can't imagine going back into the closet for any reason. Hiding who I am after all I've fought for feels like a betrayal of my true self."

"It won't be like that, I promise. We've managed our relationship pretty well so far. It hasn't felt like a betrayal, has it?"

"No, but what about our future? Does this mean we can't be out in public together? Or worse, that we can never live together?"

"Let's cross that bridge when we get there. For now, can't we just live in the present? Let's be thankful for what we have."

"I am thankful for you, Scott. But I don't get how this can work. Have you ever considered leaving the Navy?"

"To be honest? No. As a career, it's all I've ever dreamed of," Scott admitted. "And it's not that simple. I signed a contract. I owe them years of service before I could do that."

"I never thought about that." Michael shook his head. "This changes everything about our future. I'm not sure what to think."

"Understood. Promise me you'll think about this. Let's not make any rash decisions, OK?"

Michael nodded, and they strolled.

•••

They continued to make their way toward the monument in silence. Some of the heaviness abated, and against his better judgment, Scott took Michael's hand in his—he only hoped no one recognized him. Whatever the risk, he needed to bridge the distance between them. Michael squeezed his hand in return but didn't turn to look at him. Still, Scott took it as a good sign.

As they wandered, Scott knew they were on unsteady ground, and he wasn't sure how to fix it. Michael's questions weren't unreasonable. Scott had the same concerns. How could they lead a normal life if they could never live together? He couldn't think about that now. He was simply grateful there was still hope for them. Scott also understood that Michael might not want to continue their relationship as it had been. It was uncharacteristic of him, but he had to explain what was in his heart.

"Michael, these past six months have been the best in my life, and it's because of you. You light up my world with unexpected silliness and laughter. You've made my arduous med school experience bearable and removed my loneliness. I feel fully alive when I'm with you. I'm not ready to give up on us. I hope you aren't either."

"How do you do that?" Michael asked.

"What do you mean? Do what?"

"Make me melt with your words? I am so angry with you, yet you make me want to hug and kiss you and never let you go. How do you do that?"

"It's you, Michael. I've never felt this for anyone else before. If

my words cause you to feel that way, it's only because you have tapped a spring deep within me. It's all you."

The look on Michael's face blocked out all his fears. He gazed up at Scott with wide eyes filled with devotion. It was as if Michael had opened his heart to him despite his deception. Scott hadn't planned on saying I love you, but now that he did, something inside him changed. Scott realized that words were not enough—especially considering the sacrifice he was asking of Michael. Scott was not one for grand gestures, but at that moment, he was overcome with adoration for this sweet, idealistic man. He couldn't bear losing him. Then, not caring who might see them, Scott leaned in and kissed Michael passionately.

Fuck it. This is what I want to do. I don't care who sees us.

CHAPTER ELEVEN
GIVING IT A GO
1984

    His second year of med school proved more challenging than the first. There was little time for anything but studying. Scott's courses were fascinating, and he enthusiastically dove into each new area. Unlike his first year, Scott participated in study groups and sought the intellectual stimulation of his classmates. Competition was ever-present among them, but Scott was never one to shy away from a fight. Sparring with other second-year students was one of his favorite pastimes.

    His second year also brought clinical experience. Interviewing patients, performing initial examinations, and diagnosing was thrilling. Despite the long road ahead, Scott felt like a doctor. In addition to his classwork, he and many of his classmates volunteered at nearby clinics to gain more experience. Scott was mentally and physically drained by the end of the week, but he loved every minute.

    Unfortunately, more time on campus and in the clinic meant fewer trips to D.C. to visit Michael. Grateful that Michael had given him a second chance, Scott was overly solicitous when they were together. Although it was difficult, he committed to visiting him each Saturday night. He brought his books, and if the schedule allowed, he'd

stay overnight so they could spend the next day studying. On those rare occasions, Michael practically danced around the apartment, singing to himself. They fell into a comfortable rhythm together. On those Sundays, it almost felt as if they were living together. Scott knew it was the closest they could come to Michael's dream. He loved spending ordinary time together, not having to entertain one another or go out. Simply having Michael in the room made Scott feel secure.

Nine months into their relationship, Scott believed he and Michael had a future together. Once out of med school, he could be assigned to serve at a Naval hospital anywhere in the United States. He hoped Michael would be willing to move wherever he was stationed. We'll have to be discreet, he thought. Michael could have his own apartment. Then Scott could spend all his free time with him. Of course, they couldn't be seen as a couple in public. But he hoped Michael would get used to that.

Ever since the big blowup, they stealthily avoided any detailed discussion of the future. Way too much was unknown, and both wanted to enjoy the present. Scott did not press Michael for a commitment or questions about the future. That would invite a conversation neither of them was ready to have.

Coming out to Glen proved to be one of his best decisions. They were fast friends from the start, and this cemented their relationship. They shared their frustrations with the Navy, especially with the ban on gays in the military.

"Do you think they'll ever get rid of the ban?" Scott asked.

"I do. It already seems like they've stopped hunting us down," Glen replied. "Hell, I've actually seen a couple of guys out in Dupont Circle."

"Aren't you worried they'll say something? You need to be more careful."

"Look, man, if they're at the bars, they have as much to lose as I do. After a nod of the head, we don't interact at all."

"I guess it's better that way," Scott thought aloud. "Then there's no guilt by association if they're ever found out."

"Right. But, dude, you've got to lighten up. It's like you're

obsessed with being caught. Anyone we meet when we go out is also putting himself in jeopardy. You need to loosen up. Let yourself have a little fun."

"You might be right, Glen. Thank God we've got each other. I really can't have this conversation with Michael. He doesn't get it."

"And he likely never will. You should be more like me. It's way less complicated when you only sleep with a guy once. No strings attached."

"That says more about your inability to commit than anything else."

They laughed it off, both clear on how very different they were. In contrast to Scott, Glen was a free spirit—although he was careful to remain secretive. He'd often relieve Scott's worries and get him out of his head. Scott had someone to confide in for the first time in his life. Scott poured his heart out when things got complicated with Michael. Their deepened friendship was a lifeline for both.

Soon, a quartet formed: Scott, Michael, Glen, and Ted. After the latter two slept together a few times, they became the perfect wingmen for each other in pursuing new conquests at the clubs. Scott had a small gay community for the first time, and he loved it.

•••

Michael adjusted his expectations regarding his relationship with Scott. He had a choice: either break up with Scott because of the double life he led or learn to live with it. Their first anniversary was approaching, and Michael was unwilling to let go of this man he'd fallen in love with. Together with Ted and Glen, they had formed a little gay family. They'd often take turns cooking meals for special occasions and holidays. If they couldn't be together on the actual days, they'd be sure to plan a gathering to mark birthdays or holidays.

However, the landscape had changed for gay men. The AIDS crisis was in full swing, and Michael worried about Ted and Glen, neither of whom could seem to settle down with a steady boyfriend. They were young and healthy men—their sense of invincibility could not be curbed. Michael asked Scott to talk to Ted, who was as popular with the boys as ever. Try as he might, Ted didn't seem to take his medical advice seriously.

"Ted, I'm worried about you," Michael said, watching the latest stud leave their apartment.

"What? Don't be silly. I'm fine."

"I hope you're being careful. Scott says we should use condoms."

"Come on, that's only if you're a bottom. You know me. I'm always on top."

"You are not! And that's not true, Ted. There's a risk either way. Please promise me you'll be more careful."

"Yes, mother hen," he said, wrestling Michael into a hug. "You love me, don't you? It's so sweet how you worry about me."

They had that conversation repeatedly, but Ted never seemed to take it as seriously. The crisis cast a shadow over the party atmosphere at the clubs and within the gay community. Despite the news about AIDS, these men were the closest thing Michael had to having his own family. As he reflected on their lives, Michael could picture a future together. As much as he wanted a home of their own, he had grown accustomed to their routine. The idea of continuing as they were did not seem as awful as it once seemed. It was a compromise, to be sure, but perhaps it was worth it, especially if it was the only way he and Scott could be together.

The challenges continued to mount when spring rolled around. Both he and Scott were facing finals. Michael's degree program was reaching its end, culminating in brutally difficult comprehensive exams. Seeing each other every week proved challenging. With all the demands on their time and the stress of both clinical and academic programs, neither had much emotional energy to spare. They didn't read too much into their minor squabbles or impatience. But there was an obvious strain on their relationship.

As graduation approached, Michael cast a wide net by sending his applications to schools all over the D.C., Maryland, and Virginia areas. He even applied to an independent school near his hometown in Roanoke. However, Michael was confident something would materialize closer to D.C. He hoped he and Ted would get jobs in D.C. and keep their apartment. But Michael worried as May turned to June, and several interviews yielded nothing. Would he have to move back home if he couldn't find a job? He couldn't even entertain that thought. That's when

he got a call from a prestigious school in Virginia.

CHAPTER TWELVE
LIFE IN VIRGINIA
1985

Michael found a one-bedroom apartment less than three miles from the high school campus. It was only a twenty-minute drive from his childhood home, but it provided the independence he needed. Michael was glad to live near his parents and siblings but happy to have his own place. His parents had given him an old table and chairs for the kitchen, and he used wooden wine boxes as bookshelves. He took pride in his apartment and invited old high school friends for drinks or dinner. Roanoke could not rival Washington, D.C., as a city, but Michael believed he could call it home.

When the job offer from North Cross School came through, he was shocked. It was the most highly-ranked independent school in the area. Most of the other private schools were conservative Christian schools. No way he would work at one of those. Michael would have to test the waters about coming out at North Cross. But the likelihood of getting fired for being gay was far lower than at the Christian schools. He and Scott hoped he'd get a job closer to D.C., but nothing had come through. Besides, he reasoned, he could never afford to live there on a teacher's salary.

Scott generously offered to help him move and drove the four and a half hours from Baltimore. The drive south was beautiful, and they stopped along the way to take in the countryside. As they neared the area where he grew up, Michael explained every historical detail and recounted stories about his childhood.

"OK, so this is the high school. Look how tiny it is. Can you believe I spent four years there?"

"Actually, no. I can't imagine being gay in such a small school."

"Oh, I wasn't out back then. I would have been destroyed," Michael exclaimed. "I didn't even realize I was gay until I went away to college."

"This area is quite bucolic. I really feel like I'm in the Deep South," Scott said.

"Well, it's not the Deep South, but it's a different world here."

"Should I be worried about you?"

"Hell no! I grew up here, and I know how to play the game. But I am hoping to make a difference in the lives of young people grappling with their sexuality."

"Then being a counselor at this fancy high school sounds like a perfect fit. It's just that it's so far away."

"It is. That is going to suck. With med school continuing to demand more and more of your time, I'd be a distraction. You need to stay focused on that. We'll have to make the best of the times we can spend together."

"Look at you being the responsible one! You're such an adult, Michael."

"Fuck you!"

He laughed at the playful jibe. Michael believed that this was the right move. He couldn't entertain the thought of being unemployed. His parents stressed the importance of hard work to secure a stable future. If he had to move far from Scott to get a job, so be it.

•••

Ted was not pleased with Michael's move to Roanoke. Best of friends, they were more than roommates, and Ted never saw it coming.

"How could you leave Washington, D.C., for a tiny town in Virginia? I mean, are there any gay folks there at all?" Ted asked.

"Of course, there are, Ted. You'll see when you come to visit me. It's not that far away."

"Are you kidding? I wouldn't be caught dead in the South. You know what they do to us gay boys down there. D.C. is the furthest south I go."

"Come on. It's not like I'm moving to the backwoods. Roanoke is a nice little city. It even has a gay bar."

"Goodness gracious! A true-to-life gay bar? Well then, I'm sold."

Ted and Michael argued about leaving D.C. over and over again. When his mocking went nowhere, Ted attempted to persuade Michael. He promised to cover his rent until a job came through. It was a generous offer. Ted was nearly begging him to stay. And as tempting as it was, Michael hated the idea of being unemployed. Throughout his life, his parents had instilled in him the value of hard work. A steady job with medical insurance was held up as the goal. When his father got laid off during Michael's teens, the family struggled to make ends meet. Images of his parents at the kitchen table floated through his mind. Paper and pen in hand, they calculated every penny from week to week, deciding which bills to pay and those that could wait. There were no dinners out, not even trips to McDonald's. They made do with frayed clothing and simple meals. Michael could never allow that to happen. He was offered an excellent job at an elite school. Although it was far from his life in D.C., it was the right thing to do.

Although there were promises to visit each other often, they rarely met. They spoke on the phone every week, sharing Ted's latest conquest or romantic drama. Michael filled him in on life in his small town and his new career. Despite the distance, their friendship was as tight as ever. Their conversations proved to be more substantial than when living together. Michael shared his concerns about HIV and Ted's revolving door of suitors.

"Ted, when will you settle down and get a boyfriend?"

"Me, settle down? Do you know who you're talking to? Besides, I am having the time of my life."

"What about love? Don't you want something deeper than a one-night stand?"

"Honey, I believe you're projecting," Ted replied. "You're pining

away down there in Virginia—no Scott, no sex, no life. When will you realize that you belong back here in D.C.?"

"You may be right, but I love my job. And you need to be more careful. I hope you are being safe. You're playing a dangerous game of Russian roulette."

"And you worry too much."

"I don't think so, Ted. Have you been tested?"

"No. I'm fine. And you need to stop nagging me."

"You know, if we were still living together, I'd have taken you to the clinic long ago," Michael said.

"Yes, but you abandoned me for the backwoods and that navy man of yours."

"Well, I hardly see him anymore either."

"Does that mean I have a chance?"

"Seriously, Ted? I was head over heels for you, but all you could think about was your next piece of man meat. You're such a tease."

"I am a tease, but I always thought you and I would end up together after I got all this out of my system."

"Clearly, you have a lot more left in that system of yours," Michael said. He was shocked by Ted's revelation. "And what's with your unrequited love for me? Now that I'm miles away from you and in a serious relationship?"

"Oh, don't get your panties in a bunch. You and Scott won't last, but I'll still be here, perhaps a little worse for the wear."

"You mean like a worn-out queen?"

"Hey, easy there. I've got a lot more miles on me yet. And I'm certainly not ready to settle down."

Ted was his best friend, and his casual mention of his feelings for Michael didn't go unnoticed. *If I was single and living in D.C., could we actually be a couple?* he wondered. He loved Ted, but not as profoundly as Scott. However, after all his insecurity back during grad school, Ted's admission made him feel good. *I guess I'm not so bad after all,* he thought.

•••

Both Michael and Scott found their daily lives more and more

demanding. Med school consumed Scott's every waking hour, and Michael knew it had to be so. He also realized that working at a private school often interfered with his personal life. There were frequent evening and weekend events at which his presence was required. Curriculum nights and college admissions fairs were typical. Michael's attendance at sporting events, concerts, or plays, while not required, was highly recommended. The administration noticed who wasn't there. Not that he minded being on campus.

Michael loved his job and enjoyed supporting his students. By the end of his first year, he realized that Scott's visits had become less frequent. He couldn't blame him. Michael had only driven up to Baltimore twice. Strangely, Michael was not upset about it. He was so immersed in his role at North Cross that there was little time for anything else. Besides the fact that he was hours away from Scott, it was a dream job. Michael wasn't conscious that they had drifted apart over that last year. They still loved each other, but it was apparent that life was taking them down very different paths.

Their calls became less and less frequent. They still got together for special occasions and holidays, but it wasn't enough. Those moments underscored the distance between them. It was then that Michael missed the dinners after work or weekends spent studying. Those ordinary moments made him feel they were a couple—that they weren't simply dating. He hoped they could settle into their old routine after Scott finished med school. But Michael couldn't blame it all on Scott. His own schedule consumed his every waking hour.

Michael enjoyed the popularity a young new teacher gained from his high school students. His days were fully booked, with kids seeking relationship advice or help with anxiety. The juniors and seniors sought him out as they began the college application process. Michael was never bored at North Cross.

As year one turned to two and three, Michael built a reputation as a trustworthy adult that students could rely on for help. He relished every encounter and couldn't get enough. After testing the waters with the administration, he pinned information for gay support groups on his bulletin board and placed pamphlets explaining HIV/AIDS in his office.

It started as a trickle but became a steady stream of students confiding in him about sexual identity. He truly felt that he was making a difference.

However, one area of Michael's life wasn't fulfilled. He was lonely and missed his gay family back in D.C. During his first year at North Cross, Michael barely had the energy to think about guys. But now that he was established and comfortable in his routine, he ached for human touch. He longed to be with other gay people. There was a small gay bar in Roanoke called The Last Straw. The one-story brick building was nondescript, with a long wooden bar spanning the room. It was famous for its cruising scene. Michael planned to go dozens of times but always lost his nerve. The only thing he hated more than hanging out in bars was going alone. Sadly, gay bars were the only places he could meet other gay men.

Sitting in his car outside the bar, Michael watched guys walk in and out. There was nothing to be intimidated about, he reasoned. After fifteen minutes sitting there, he checked his hair in the mirror and ambled to the entrance. The bouncer checked his ID and smiled at him.

"Fresh blood! Welcome to The Last Straw. It's nice to see a new face. I'm sure you'll get lots of attention tonight."

"Thanks. I could use an ego boost," Michael mumbled.

"Oh, with that face and those eyes, you'll get much more than a boost. Go have fun."

The music was loud, and the drinks were strong. Plastered all over the walls were posters encouraging safe sex, and a bowl of condoms sat on the bar. In a few short years, the AIDS epidemic had become the central focus of the gay community. After getting a drink, Michael stood and read an advertisement for the Blue Ridge Lambda Alliance.

"You interested in becoming a volunteer?"

"What? Oh, yeah. I think so. I'm Michael."

"Hank. Nice to meet you. I work at the BRLA, and we always look for volunteers."

"I'd love to learn more about what you do," Michael said.

"The BRLA is one of the area's few care and advocacy organizations. We connect people with health services, counseling, and basic companionship outlets."

"I'm a counselor at a local high school. Do you need counselors?"

"Are you kidding?" Hank said as he put his arm around him and explained what they needed.

Michael sat at the bar with Hank until late in the evening, laughing and carrying on. When they announced the last call, Hank pulled Michael into him.

"Hey, let's go to my place for a little fun. I'm just a few blocks away."

Michael was more than tempted. He hadn't seen Scott in months, and Hank's sexy charm enchanted him. Rarely had Michael connected with anyone at a gay bar. Why not go for it? Who's to know? But Michael's guilt got the best of him.

"I'd love to, Hank. But I'm in a relationship, albeit a long-distance one."

"My loss, for sure," Hank responded. "Maybe I'll see you at BRLA?"

"Absolutely. I need to get more involved with the gay community here in Roanoke."

Before long, Michael could be seen at the center three or four days a week. He answered phones, visited with clients, and offered his counseling services pro bono. He learned how little funding AIDS research was getting and helped lobby local politicians. Michael rekindled his love of activism and sought to do more.

CHAPTER THIRTEEN
THE TALK
1986

Scott could hardly believe that four years of med school were behind him. Residency was right around the corner, and he was eager to begin practicing. However, Scott no longer had the cover of med school. After residency, the Navy would station him somewhere to begin his years of service. He couldn't avoid the issue any longer. Scott knew he had to have the dreaded discussion about their future with Michael.

He planned to drive down to Roanoke right after final exams. It had been several months since they had seen each other. Even their phone calls had become less frequent. Regardless of how busy they both were, Scott couldn't help but believe they were drifting apart. The very thought broke his heart.

Standing at the door, Scott felt beads of sweat drip from his temples. Why am I so nervous? It's only Michael. But he knew better than that. This visit would likely determine their future, and Scott was unsure if they would come out of it unscathed. Finally, he rang the bell, and the door opened. A smiling face greeted him, and his worries melted away.

"Oh my God, it's good to see you," Michael exclaimed as he

pulled him into the apartment. "Can I give the good doctor a kiss?"

"I'm not a doctor yet, and you had better. I'm about to burst with anticipation."

"Is that so, Dr. Scott? Perhaps we should go into the bedroom. I believe I require an examination."

"I believe you are long overdue for an injection, young Michael."

Clothes were shed hastily, and months of pent-up sexual frustration burst forth. Scott kissed Michael's neck and chest as he worked his way from his nipples to his abs. He looked up at Michael just before he engulfed him. Michael moaned in ecstasy and laced his fingers through Scott's jet-black hair. His short military cut made it difficult to grab onto as he pushed himself further down Scott's throat. It was getting hot way too fast, and Scott pulled away.

"I want to be inside you—now."

Michael reached into the nightstand and pulled out a condom without losing eye contact with Scott.

"Go easy, tiger. It's been a very long time."

Scott lifted Michael's legs and kissed him gently as he pressed forward. Slowly, he let himself be consumed by Michael's warmth. Then he rested his muscular chest against Michael's, lying motionless, savoring the feeling of their joined bodies. Scott began to move, and soon, their bodies found their usual rhythm. He looked down at Michael with adoration.

"I love you, Michael. I dreamed about this every night I spent without you."

Michael pulled Scott's head down into a deep kiss, and they let themselves be carried away by their passion. When they were finished, they both let out a cackle.

"Well, that was energetic," Michael said.

"I'm wiped out now. I'm not sure I can move."

"You? I'll be lucky if I can walk after the way you rode me, partner."

"Hey, I simply followed your lead, Mr. Power Bottom!"

Their playful banter kept them entertained while they regained enough strength to take a shower. Their old familiarity returned, and

Scott felt more confident about their impending conversation.

\#

Michael was pleasantly surprised by their impassioned reunion. Given that their communication had cooled over the last six months, he didn't know what to expect. He was heartened because the spark was still there. Their lovemaking was more intense than usual, but that wasn't what struck him most. Michael felt as if they were finally coming back home—reconnecting after a long hiatus. There was a glimmer of hope for their future.

The following morning, Michael rose early to prepare breakfast. He quietly padded out to the kitchen to brew the coffee, fry some crispy bacon, and prepare Scott's favorite, eggs Benedict. When Scott poked his head out of the bedroom, pots and pans were piled in the sink, grease was splattered all over the stovetop, and Michael had hollandaise sauce dripping from the tip of his nose.

"Good morning, handsome," Scott said as he moved in for a kiss. Michael lifted his head to meet Scott's lips but felt his tongue on his nose instead. "Yum. I've never had Michael Benedict. Perhaps I should pour more hollandaise on you and lap it up."

"Yuck. That sounds disgusting. Why don't you pour yourself a cup of coffee while I make your plate?"

"I could get used to this. Looks like you've been a busy beaver."

"This is only the beginning. I have a great day planned," Michael said as he placed Scott's breakfast before him. "Do you have sneakers or good walking shoes?"

"Sure do. Why?"

"We're going to hike the Appalachian Trail. There's a gorgeous spot called McAfee Knob. You'll be floored by it."

"I know a knob I'm floored by. Perhaps I can explore that one right now."

"Eat your breakfast, you little piggy," Michael said, giggling. "We'll have plenty of time for that after our hike."

The Appalachian Trail did not disappoint. The views of the Blue Ridge Mountains were stunning. The early summer weather provided brilliant sunshine and warmth. Their muscles burned as they climbed

to nearly 3200 feet. McAfee knob is at the top of Catawba Mountain, a strenuous hike, but the payoff was spectacular.

"This is unbelievable," Scott exclaimed. "There's a 360-degree view of all the mountains."

"I know, right!? This is only my second time here, and it's as spectacular as the first time."

They took in the natural beauty in relative silence. They were content to be in each other's company as they marveled at the sights before them. Michael then spread a blanket and unpacked a picnic lunch.

"Wow, you've thought of everything, haven't you?"

"I wanted today to be special for us. It's been way too long since we've been together."

"Just being with you is special, Michael. It really is."

Uncorking a bottle of wine, Michael poured two glasses. He unwrapped several cheeses and set out succulent grapes. They dug into their food, but there was very little chatter. They listened to the birds singing and the wind whistling through the hills. Looking over at Scott, Michael could tell he was anxious. Several times, it seemed as if he was about to say something but stopped himself.

"What's on your mind, Scott? I can almost see the gears spinning in your brain."

"You read me so well. I don't know how to approach this, but I know we have to discuss it."

"You mean our future. Well, I suppose we've avoided it as long as possible."

"Over the last few years, we have both made choices that have affected our relationship—some of them have not been so good. There have been so many circumstances out of our control," Scott said.

"Like my job being hours away from you? Or the inevitable assignment that has always loomed like a storm cloud over our future?"

"Exactly. I was so nervous about this weekend together, Michael. After so little contact, I wondered if you had moved on."

"Honestly, I wondered the same thing. Strangely, we both let that happen. But after last night, it's obvious that our feelings still run deep."

"The question is, will that be enough to carry us through this next phase?"

"It's about to get even more difficult for us, right?" Michael asked.

"More than you know. Things have gotten much too scary for gay people in the military. We all hoped that the ban would have been eliminated by now. Instead, it feels as if there is a witch hunt. Everyone is running scared."

"Are you running scared too?"

"I hate to admit it, but yes. After residency, the Navy will assign me to serve my required years of duty. When that happens, I won't have the freedom I've had during my studies. I'll likely live on a base, and they'll be able to watch my comings and goings."

"And that will make it nearly impossible for us to be together."

"Not impossible, but certainly less frequent. We'll have to be much more careful in public, and there won't be many overnight visits."

"I see. Not much of a life, is it?" Michael said. "You know, it's been so difficult being apart these last couple of years. I've often wondered if perhaps our relationship had run its course. I don't know how we'll sustain this relationship if we know it will get worse."

"I can't imagine what it's been like for you here in this small town. You've found some friends, but it must have been pretty lonely."

"It has, and it's made me realize that I don't want this kind of life. You know I love my job at the school, and I often want to share what happened or process with you. It's not necessarily the major events that I miss. It's not having someone to go shopping with or watch TV with. Ultimately, when I crawl into my bed at night, I'm painfully alone."

"I get that, Michael. I miss those Sunday afternoons hanging out at your place."

"The thing is, I need a partner who is with me, someone to come home to every night. Scott, I live alone, and as much as I know you love me, you are hours away. Now we're faced with the fact that you may be even farther away and that we will probably see each other less. What kind of life is that for a couple?"

"It's going to be challenging, for sure. But we can do it."

"I'm not so sure, Scott. I love you—you know that—but this is not the life I want. I feel more alone pining for you than when I was single."

"I get it. I miss you, too. But I have no choice in the Navy. I was fortunate enough to be sent to med school right after Annapolis. They have a right to expect that I will repay them with service. It's only right."

"That makes perfect sense—for you. It's one reason I love you. You are a man of honor. You will always do the right thing. But have you truly asked yourself if this is fair to me?"

"Of course I have, Michael. But isn't being together worth the sacrifice?"

"For you, it is. You have always wanted to be a Navy officer and doctor. You'll have that and a secret boyfriend."

"You make it sound like you're the only one suffering here. It kills me to be apart from you. But I believe we can have it all—just not in a traditional sense."

"But, Scott, I don't think I can do that with you. I'm sorry, but I can't put my life on hold until I can see you again. I hate living in the shadows, fearing that someone will discover us. It makes me feel like we are doing something dirty, illegal, or immoral. I can't feel that way about being gay. I've lived too many years with guilt and self-hatred. Not being out to my family or my co-workers only emphasizes the point. I can't go back there. I need to be out of the closet. Proud of who I am and who I love. I can never have that with you."

"I'm sorry, Michael. I know what you're saying. But please don't give up on us. We can make it work. Please, can we at least try it?"

"Scott, this is the toughest decision I've ever made. I must be true to myself, love myself, and act with integrity. I can't do that if I'm hiding. I just can't."

"Look, we've made it this long," Scott pleaded. "My service is five years. Can we at least try to make it through that? Then we can be together."

"Do you hear yourself? You're asking me to put my life on hold for another five years," Michael said. "I've always wanted this to work. God knows I've really tried. I will always love you, Scott. But it's time

to let go."

"So that's it, then?" Scott asked, tears welling in his eyes. "We're done?"

With tears streaming down his cheeks, Michael nodded his head and turned toward McAfee Knob. One of the most important lessons he had learned by counseling his high school students was that they had to be true to themselves. His heart ached at the thought of losing Scott, especially after their passionate reunion. At that moment, something profound revealed itself—Michael needed to own up to the man he had become. There could be no more hiding in the closet, even for the man he loved. This was not how he imagined today would turn out so much for his romantic picnic. Scott put his arm around his shoulder, took his thumb, and wiped the tears from Michael's eyes.

"I'm sorry, Michael. Sorry, I can't be what you want me to be."

A single tear fell from Scott's eye, but Michael turned away. He couldn't bear seeing Scott's pain while bearing his own. They stood looking at the spectacular view before them as they silently mourned the end of their relationship.

CHAPTER FOURTEEN
MICHAEL IN SAN FRANCISCO
1988

  After his breakup with Scott, Michael tried to get more involved with the Blue Ridge Lambda Alliance. But he was always afraid someone from his past would spot him, or worse, a family member. Michael just couldn't capture the freedom he felt while living in Washington, D.C. In his little suburb of Roanoke, he was near to his family and old high school friends. He loved being close by to play with nephews and nieces or hang with his old buddies. But he wasn't out to them. It was a small, conservative town that equated being gay with going to hell. Michael was not ready to risk losing his family by coming out. The more time he spent in his hometown, the more complacent he became with his double life.
  He felt like a hypocrite. He broke up with Scott because they could not live as an openly gay couple. Yet here he was, hiding in plain sight among everyone he knew. He was incensed when he saw the news coverage of the Pride parade in San Francisco on the local news station. Typical of the conservative slant, the newscaster made disparaging remarks about the depraved behavior of homosexuals in San Francisco. The images shown were of drag queens, men in chaps, and "dykes on

bikes." They made sure to select the more inflammatory clips to drive home the message that gay people were freaks. He hated that he lived in a place where prejudice against gay people was so blatant and accepted. But as he watched the coverage, he realized San Francisco not only accepted but celebrated all facets of the gay community. In that instant, he knew what he had to do.

What am I doing here? I can never be who I am without being judged. It's time for a change.

Michael drove to D.C. to see Ted. During their recent phone calls, they both expressed dissatisfaction with their jobs, friends, and lack of lovers. Michael hoped Ted would join him on his new adventure, but he hadn't mentioned his idea on the phone. Michael wanted to see Ted's face when he told him of his plan to move to San Francisco.

Michael sat at the table at Mr. Henry's, waiting for his best friend to arrive. Ted was known for his entrances, not for punctuality. Michael's leg jiggled under the table in anticipation. He could hardly wait. He glanced at the door and spotted a gaunt figure walking in. There was no huge smile or squealing at their long-awaited reunion. Michael stood with his mouth agape as Ted approached the table.

"Hey, stranger," Ted said with a sad smile.

Michael didn't have to ask. He knew what was wrong—a cold, steel hand squeezed his heart. No, no, not Ted.

"Ted, why didn't you tell me?"

"On the phone? I couldn't bear it. The look on your face is hard enough."

"I'm sorry. I didn't mean to stare. I don't know what to say. I'm..." His voice trailed off.

Ted told him of his diagnosis and his trials during the last month. His tone belied the hopelessness just beneath the surface. He had been lucky thus far—no serious opportunistic infections, just weight loss and a cough that wouldn't go away. Michael tried to be optimistic, but they both knew better. What they didn't know was how much time he had left. It was different for everyone. Michael's big news wasn't as important anymore. Ted tried to sound supportive and excited, but it fell flat.

"That's fabulous, Michael. Thank God you're finally getting out

of that hillbilly town."

"Why don't you come with me, Ted?"

"Nah, I'm not up for such a big move. I have my doctors here and all."

"Come on, maybe a change in scenery is just what you need. Besides, I'm sure San Francisco has the best doctors for HIV."

They both knew he wouldn't make the move, but Michael tried to persuade him. At the end of the day, they parted. Michael held his friend longer than was comfortable. He didn't want to let go.

"Enough already. Go—start your new life and try not to be such a good boy."

The image of Ted remained in his mind. He couldn't believe his beautiful friend had HIV. Michael just hoped he'd have years, not months, to live. Fuck this goddamned disease! He screamed as tears streamed down his face.

•••

By the end of the summer, he was driving across the country to start a new life. Leaving North Cross and his beloved students proved heart-wrenching, but he hoped to find a home in a similar school in the Bay Area. Everyone back home thought he was crazy to leave behind all he knew and loved. To them, he was making a rash decision. Only Michael understood that if he didn't get out of his small town, he would shrivel up and die. Starting a new life across the country was a perfect way to get over his breakup with Scott. He needed a fresh start. San Francisco allowed him to be fully out of the closet. There would be no hiding any longer.

There were very few things that Michael was sure about when he moved to San Francisco. However, he promised himself he would not live his life in the closet. Michael planned to join the San Francisco Gay Men's Chorus. He believed it would offer him a less intimidating way of meeting men. He had no desire to repeat the barhopping he and Ted did in D.C. The chorus offered him something more than a social outlet. It offered him a community.

His first performance with the chorus changed something in him. Michael felt it deep within his chest—almost as if his heart had

burst open and his true essence was spewing forth. Fire leaped from his core, and every inch of his body buzzed. Standing surrounded by gay men, a crowd of people smiling at him while he sang, he knew his life would never be the same. They were at the San Francisco City Hall, and the Gay Men's Chorus was performing for a gala event. As one of the shorter men, he stood front and center on the grand staircase, directly under the cupola. Taking in the sights and sounds around him, he began to sing with greater force, hardly able to hold back his exuberance when the refrain rolled around.

We're all here together, whatever story we bring.
Pride makes us step forward.
We're gay men, and we're here to sing.
Diversity makes us strong.

He felt every phrase, every word pulse through his veins as the harmony swirled around him. His body and mind were thrumming, and he felt fully alive for the very first time. Never had he stood in public and proclaimed that he was gay. And although he didn't know a soul in that room, aside from the acquaintances he had in the chorus, Michael knew he would never forget that moment.

Michael was lost in his thoughts when the crowd erupted in thunderous applause and startled him out of his reverie. Looking out at the smiling faces, he nearly broke down and cried. Freedom washed over him, melting the chill of his fear—fear of rejection, fear of abandonment, fear of violence.

When the performance was over, Michael milled about, grabbing a glass of wine and a nibble of cheese. He wished there was someone with whom to share his bursting heart. He was so new to the city that he hadn't made any friends yet. Scanning the reception area, he spotted doors to a balcony overlooking United Nations Plaza. He ambled over and stood gazing at the twinkling lights of his new city by the bay. *Someone pinch me. Is this really happening?* he thought. *My life is finally beginning. No more hiding who I am from my family and friends. I am starting my life in San Francisco with a clean slate.* Although Michael had come out to a small circle of friends, most of them back home didn't know he was gay. He vowed that as he met his new community of friends, he would

identify as gay. Coming out to his people back east would take some time, but they were thousands of miles away. For now, he took in the city that lay before him. He turned to go back inside when the San Francisco winds chilled his bones through his flimsy tuxedo. I thought California was supposed to be warm.

•••

The Gay Men's Chorus was planning a variety show—a departure from their usual choral concerts, allowing members to sing solos, duets, or any other ensemble work. The chorus comprised over one hundred singers, so this was an opportunity to shine apart from the choir. During the auditions, the conductor sat midway in the theater. As each act appeared center stage, he asked, "Is this number hot or cold?"

What? Michael had no clue what he was asking. "I'm not sure. I suppose it's hot," he replied. "It's a Steven Sondheim song, 'I Remember Sky.'"

"A ballad then—it's cold. It won't get the audience tapping its toes and on the edge of their seats," Dr. Hill replied. "All right, go ahead. Show us what you've got."

Michael was disheartened by Hill's tepid reaction, but he sang with as much passion as he could muster.

"Very nice, Michael. I'm not familiar with that song. Plan on singing it for the show. Next."

Thrilled, Michael took a seat in the auditorium. He loved hearing what the other guys were singing. After a few upbeat numbers, he realized what the director was after. The acts with a bit of comedy or choreography garnered a generous response from the audience. Those were the hot numbers, entertaining and funny. He chided himself for choosing a serious song. As that thought swirled in his mind, he heard a melody from Les Miserables. "On My Own" was one of his favorite love songs from the show. Standing on stage was a guy he had a crush on—Joey stood with his arms held out, longing for someone to love him. The lyrics came alive through his rich, baritone voice.

On my own
Pretending he's beside me
All alone,
I walk with him till morning
Without him,
I feel his arms around me
And when I lose my way, I close my eyes
And he has found me.
– Les Misérables

Michael's heart melted. Gazing up at the stage, he felt as if Joey were singing to him—that they were the only two people in the room. Even though it was a ballad, not a toe-tapping hot number, the audience erupted in applause. Joey bowed and made his way back to his seat. Michael had to meet him. Since he didn't have Ted as his wingman, Michael gathered his courage as he rose from his seat and walked over to him. He held out his hand and introduced himself.

"Hi, I'm Michael. I have to tell you—you were phenomenal. Your voice is like a balm to a lonely heart."

"Wow, thank you. That is certainly poetic. I'm Joey; come sit."

"Seriously, Joey. You had the whole place wrapped around your finger. And it wasn't just your voice. The way you communicated the angst of unrequited love was powerful."

"I need to hang out with you all the time. You are great for my ego."

After auditions, Michael and Joey headed to the Castro to grab a drink. They ended up spending the entire evening together. They were a sight to behold. Joey had long black hair tied in a ponytail, a red bandana covered his head, and he wore ripped jeans with a threadbare t-shirt. His silver-blue eyes were piercing. Michael was enchanted as he hung on his every word. Michael was preppy as could be: a pink Oxford shirt, khakis, and Docksider shoes with no socks. It wasn't just how they dressed—they couldn't be more different. Michael was drawn to Joey's bohemian look and vision. He was an actor starring in a gay production at a tiny theater south of Market. Michael was star-struck.

Tilting Toward the Sun 83

"I'm sorry to see the evening end," Joey said as last call was announced.

"Yeah, me too. I'm sorry if I talked your ear off for the last few hours."

"I think we both did our share of talking," Joey responded. "Listen, I'd love to see you again. What do you say we meet for brunch on Sunday? At the Patio Cafe?"

"I'd love that. Is eleven o'clock good for you?"

"Perfect. It was really wonderful to spend the evening with you, Michael. See you soon, then."

Michael moved in for a hug, but Joey kissed him directly on the lips, then hugged him tightly. Michael barely contained his excitement. He wanted to ask him back to his apartment but didn't want to risk being labeled a slut. He held off, at least until after the second date.

Brunch turned out even better than Michael had hoped. Joey had been living in San Francisco for several years, filling him in on the neighborhood gossip, cheap restaurants, and bars to avoid. Michael didn't know the protocol when the check came and pulled out his wallet. He assumed they'd split the bill, but when Joey didn't make a move, he realized he expected Michael to pay. Michael was very anxious about his financial situation. He had been in San Francisco for three weeks and still had no job prospects.

"So, what's on the agenda for the rest of the day? Do you have time to make the sign of the cross?"

"The sign of the cross?" Michael asked, confused. "I'm not religious."

"No, no." Joey laughed. "It's what we call bar hopping on Eighteenth and Castro Streets. We hit every bar in all four directions."

"Dude, you got me nervous. I wondered if I was back in Virginia with a religious zealot."

"Far from it. Are you game?"

"I'd love to, but I have to look for a job. Can I take a rain check?"

"Absolutely. Are you free tomorrow? I'd love a second date," Joey said.

"That would be great. I really enjoyed our time together."

"Awesome. Here's my address. Same time tomorrow?"

• • •

Joey didn't have a car, so Michael drove to an address in Noe Valley. Parking on the street, he looked up at a beautiful Victorian house perched on a hill. He looked back at the napkin on which Joey scribbled his address. Yes, this was the place. Michael scaled the many steps leading to the entrance. He had almost reached the front door when he heard Joey's voice.

"Hey, Michael. Down here."

Joey stood at a door directly below the main staircase, waving him down. Michael turned back down the stairs and joined Joey.

"That's the owner's residence. I live in this studio apartment. Come on in—I'll give you the grand tour."

"Well, that certainly makes more sense. I wondered if I had landed a date with a wealthy entrepreneur."

"Hardly!" Joey replied, laughing. "I live here rent-free in exchange for cleaning their house. And let me tell you, they are getting a great deal. It takes me hours!"

"Seriously? That's a great deal. I mean, who gets to live rent-free in San Francisco?"

"As you can see, my residence is palatial. That's the bedroom, kitchen, and living area. Oh, and a bathroom—all in five hundred square feet."

"Cozy. But it's free."

They spent the afternoon in the Castro and did the infamous sign of the cross. Michael was enchanted by Joey's free spirit and devil-may-care attitude. Although he had little money, he seemed as happy as could be. Michael was worried about everything. It was one of his worst attributes. Watching Joey embrace his bohemian scarcity, he believed he could learn something from him.

"Hey, I know you don't have much cash either, but why don't we splurge on a burrito for dinner? There's this yummy taco joint on Eighteenth Street called Azteca."

"I've never had a burrito, but as long as it won't break the bank, I'm willing to try," Michael said.

"Never? Then you are in for a treat. They're huge, so we can split one. It'll cost us less than two dollars each."

Joey was right. The burrito was cheap, filling, and oh-so-tasty. Michael made a mental note of Azteca. *This is a perfect place to get a good, inexpensive meal.*

CHAPTER FIFTEEN
EATING OUT
1987-1988

The Navy stationed Scott at the National Naval Medical Centers in Bethesda, Maryland, a suburb of Washington, D.C. With a specialization in infectious diseases, he was allowed privileges at George Washington University Hospital in their AIDS ward. He couldn't have dreamed of a better assignment, and he was psyched to be back in D.C. Scott was tempted to contact Michael to share his good news. He had an ember of hope that Michael might reconsider and move back to D.C. Ultimately, Scott was afraid to open that old wound. Both he and Michael had moved on—it was time for him to let go of the past.

Scott found comfort in structure and routine. His favorite restaurant became his second home—Galileo served authentic Italian cuisine with no pretense. The wait staff and owners greeted him by name and showed him to his usual table. At the end of a long day at the hospital, Galileo was what the doctor ordered. Residency had been everything he expected: double shifts, sleepless nights, and no social life. Now that he was finally a doctor, he got his life back.

"Back again, Captain? Your usual?" the server asked.

"Yes, thanks, Rick. Unless there are any specials I shouldn't miss."

"Actually, if you like it hot, there's spicy penne all'arrabbiata."

"Well, I do like it hot. But of course, anything you serve is hot," Scott said, checking the waiter's reaction. Their flirty banter had escalated recently.

"Oh, Captain, you have no idea how hot I can be," he replied with a wink.

"In that case, you'll have to join me for dinner one of these days."

"Just say the word," he said with a seductive smile. "Of course, you'll have to wait until my day off."

"And when is that?"

"Tomorrow, but perhaps we can go somewhere else? I feel like I live here."

"Great. Where shall I pick you up?"

"Oh, so then it will be a proper date? I'll be sure to get dolled up."

The following evening, Scott picked up his date and took him to a quiet French restaurant. They hit it off immediately. Rick had a playful personality that drew Scott right in. His nonstop chatter kept him entertained all evening. It had been a long time since he'd been out with a guy, and he relaxed into the relative normalcy of going on a date. Everyone at Galileo knew Scott was in the Navy, so there was no great secret to keep from Rick. There was no need to explain the need for discretion. He still bore the scars of his failed relationship with Michael, and he'd learned that being upfront about his circumstances was best.

Scott wasn't in search of a serious relationship. He didn't know if he had the emotional strength to entertain a significant commitment. Medicine and the Navy were the central components of his life—and he liked it that way. All he needed was a little companionship. Looking across the table at this delightful young man, Scott smiled. Rick had no hidden agenda, no drive to change the world—he was refreshingly uncomplicated. *Perhaps this is precisely what I need*, he thought.

"So, I suppose we can't go back to base and have sex, can we, Captain?"

"My, aren't we forward? No, there'll be no sex for us on the base. However, I have friends in the neighborhood who rent me a room."

"Well, isn't that convenient? What must a girl do to get invited to your lair?"

"I suppose you've been a good boy this evening. If you promise to be discreet, I may consider an invitation."

"Moi? I'm the height of discretion. I can play straight better than most. Yo, buddy, let's get outta this joint."

"Was that an attempt to act straight? That needs some work, young man," Scott said. "Let's get out of here and see if we can cause some trouble."

Scott's friends were seldom home. Both were congressional aides who worked hard and partied hard. They had met at the Lone Star years before. Knowing his need for secrecy, they offered him a room in their row house. They needed another housemate to help with the rent, and Scott was a perfect candidate since he was rarely there. Over the years, they had become close friends and confidants. On this fateful night, both Brian and Roland were home.

"Well, well, well, look who the cat dragged in," Brian sang as Scott and Rick walked through the door.

"Long time no see, Captain," Roland said. "And who's this tasty dish you brought to our den of iniquity?"

"Good evening, gentlemen, and I use that term loosely. This is Rick. Rick, these are my depraved housemates, Brian and Roland."

"Hi, guys. It's nice to know that Scott has actual friends. He always dines alone at Galileo."

"I thought I recognized you, Rick," Brian said. "Leave it to our resident soldier to pick up the cutest server at the place."

"Not a soldier, Brian. That's the army," Scott corrected.

"Whatever. Don't let us keep you. I'm sure you didn't come here to chat with us," Brian said, dismissing them with a wave of his hand.

"Make as much noise as you want, boys," Roland added. "We could use a little excitement in this place. It's been waaaaay too long since any of us have seen any action."

Once in the privacy of Scott's room, they fell onto the bed. The sex wasn't exactly passionate, nor was it loving. From the start, they had a playful, if superficial, relationship. They enjoyed each other's company

with no heavy expectations. It was night and day compared to the intensity of Scott's relationship with Michael. There were no profound discussions or political rants. Rick seemed content to carry on their courtship out of the spotlight. He had nothing to prove and no desire to rock the boat. Rick filled Scott's need to take care of someone, and Rick loved playing the helpless maiden, pampered and showered with gifts.

After so many years alone, Scott was a sponge, absorbing Rick's affection and need. He no longer ached for Michael. Although his relationship with Rick could not be compared with the depth of emotion he shared with Michael, he was content, perhaps even happy. He never felt like he was walking on eggshells regarding his military career. Rick accepted the limitations of their public life without question. He never sat at home pining for Scott—quite the opposite. Rick had his own life and interests to keep him busy when Scott's demanding schedule kept them apart. Scott relaxed into an easy rhythm, balancing his work at the hospital, his responsibilities at the base, and life with Rick. Things had turned out better than he ever expected.

•••

Rick brimmed with youthful energy. He planned hikes, parties, and weekend getaways. He was the perfect contrast to Scott's rigid life. Scott's world held little time for creativity or play, and Rick splashed it with color. He understood the limitations of Scott's schedule and worked around it. When the opportunity arose, he would whisk him away with a picnic basket and a bottle of wine. On the rare occasion Scott had time off, he planned trips to Rehoboth Beach in Delaware. The vibrant gay community in Rehoboth was far enough away that Scott could relax and go dancing without fear of being discovered.

At times, Scott wondered how he would keep up with him. Rick wasn't much younger but never seemed to grow out of the party boy phase. Scott watched in amazement as Rick danced into the wee hours of the morning, always the center of attention. His boyish looks garnered so much attention that Scott would sometimes slink away to get some sleep, leaving Rick to slip into bed just before sunrise. Smelling of alcohol and cigarettes, he would snuggle until Scott relented and spooned him as he drifted off to sleep.

Shortly after sunrise, Scott jogged along the shore or trail, stopped at a cafe for a muffin, and sat to read the paper. He was often halfway through his day before Rick rose from his slumber, ready to start the party all over again. Their relationship couldn't be more different from his time with Michael. Michael always searched for greater meaning and loved to analyze people's motivations. Scott enjoyed the intellectual stimulation they provided each other. But Rick was like a new puppy filled with playful energy—he kept his interactions light and superficial. Scott appreciated Rick's positivity, especially since his days at the hospital were filled with so much suffering. Coming home to Rick was like changing the channel on the TV to watch a romantic comedy or sitcom.

Within the year, Rick moved into Scott's room at Brian and Roland's house. The guys welcomed him with open arms, but not without their usual bitchy judgments.

"It's good to see you've finally gotten over Michael. Watching you mope around for months, pining after him, was getting tired," Brian said.

"And it seems you traded up—or down. Who knew you'd end up with a twink?" Roland added.

"He's only five years younger, but he has way more energy than I do," Scott admitted.

"That's hard to imagine. Perhaps it's just that your energy gets spent during your Draconian workout routine," Brian quipped.

"Although, he's not the brightest bulb on the tree," said Roland. "Smart doesn't always go hand in hand with pretty."

"You guys are impossible. He's a good guy, and we love each other. That's all that matters."

"As long as you're happy, we welcome having that tasty little eye candy gracing our humble abode," Brian said.

It was settled. Roland and Brian accepted Rick with open arms. The three of them would often go dancing when Scott was working. Together, the two couples formed a happy little family.

CHAPTER SIXTEEN
JOEY
1988

Joey and Michael spent almost every day together. The following Monday, they met downtown for the chorus rehearsal. Afterward, they went out to the Metro bar with the guys. Tongues wagged almost immediately. The new guy was sleeping with Joey. Joey pounced before anyone else had a chance. The new guy was star-struck. Michael didn't care—most of that was true. He loved hearing Joey sing, and having a boyfriend so soon after moving to the city was nice.

Since neither worked during the day, Michael spent his mornings looking through the wanted ads at Joey's place. Sometimes, he'd help Joey clean the house so that he'd get done sooner, and they could go out and play. Although he hated cleaning other people's messes, he was willing to get over his aversion if it meant that he and Joey could spend more time together.

Michael was desperate to get a job. His savings would only carry him so far. He scoured the classifieds for counseling jobs, but it was too late in the year. Most school openings were filled. So Michael cast a wider net. Community activism was at the top of his list—he hoped to work for a gay organization. He wanted to make a difference. One

morning, he spotted a position as an aide to an openly lesbian supervisor at city hall. He circled the ad and dialed the number. He drove down to city hall and filled out the application. It was a long shot, to be sure, but it was worth a try.

Later that week, Michael was helping Joey with the cleaning in the main house when he noticed a photo of two women. One of them looked familiar.

"Joey, are these the owners?"

"Yes, that's Roberta and Mary."

"Roberta Achtenberg?

"Yes, she's a city supervisor. Why?"

"I just applied for a job in her office. Do you think you could introduce us?"

"Sure, why not? I'm not sure it'll do any good, but it's worth trying."

That evening, Joey took Michael upstairs to meet Supervisor Achtenberg. Michael was excited rather than nervous. Roberta and Mary offered them wine as they sat looking out at the view of the San Francisco hills. Michael spoke of his counseling background and his desire to make a difference in the gay community in San Francisco.

"I realize this is a social visit, but I have to tell you I applied to be one of your aides. I apologize for being a giddy teenager as I wax eloquent about my hopes and dreams. But I'm so thrilled to meet you and Mary."

"Not at all," Roberta said. "I'm glad you took the initiative and that Joey introduced us. We get so many applicants that it's difficult to stand out. We're starting formal interviews next week. I'll have my assistant call to make an appointment with you."

That was all it took. The interview was like chatting with an old friend. Michael immediately hit it off with the other staffers, and by the end of the week, he had a job. Only a month after his arrival in San Francisco, Michael's life had been transformed. He was singing in the San Francisco Gay Men's Chorus, had a boyfriend, and now had a great new job.

"Let's celebrate, Joey! Let's go to Azteca. Tonight, we'll splurge.

We'll each get our own whole burrito!"

"Whoa, big spender! Don't blow it all at once!"

•••

Michael found working at city hall thrilling. Getting a job as an aide to a city supervisor was a real coup. He arrived in San Francisco during the summer of 1989 without a job, living with a roommate he had only met through a newspaper advertisement. When the staffer position popped up, it piqued his interest. Ms. Achtenberg was impressed with his volunteer work back in Virginia, and with his connection to Joey, she took a chance on him. Michael was a quick study. He threw himself into city politics, helping to draft speeches and researching data to craft policy. Before long, everyone at city hall knew the junior staffer.

The pace was exhilarating, and the hours were long. Gone were the leisurely days with Joey. Michael didn't mind the work. He loved being busy. But Joey resented Michael's time away and his tight relationship with Roberta. He was doing her laundry while his boyfriend was at her side for every meeting, cocktail party, or dinner. For the first time, Joey was embarrassed to be the house boy. He never voiced his feelings to Michael. Instead, he revealed his frustration through passive-aggressive comments and behavior.

"What? Another cocktail party with the supervisor? I should feel grateful you stopped by between events."

"I'm sorry, Joey. Her schedule is insane. I don't even have a moment for myself."

"I guess that puts me in third place—Roberta, you, then me."

"Don't do that, Joey. This is my job. Of course, you're important to me. I promise we'll do something this weekend. In fact, why don't you plan something special for us? I'll pay."

"Oh, now you're my sugar daddy?"

"That's not it at all. I only wanted us to do something nice without worrying about money. I know cash is tight. Come on; please try to understand."

"Whatever. Go back to work. I've got a show to prepare for."

They argued constantly. Ultimately, the result was the same—Michael couldn't win. If he offered to pay, Joey accused him of playing

the Daddy. When they had time together, Joey complained about all their time apart.

Michael tried his best to show Joey that he loved him, but somehow, he always came up short. He worried Joey could barely cover his bills. He had scraped together funds to buy a Vespa but didn't have enough to purchase a helmet. With little of his own money to spare, Michael bought one for him. Soon, they argued about finances. When he collected his paycheck, Joey splurged. His meager hourly wage didn't go far at the costly organic food store or Castro boutiques. Michael still kept the ethos of the working-class family that had raised him, emphasizing working hard and saving one's earnings for practical purchases. He shopped for store brands and sale items. If there were coupons available, he clipped them from the newspapers. Michael couldn't understand why Joey insisted on frequenting the most expensive stores in San Francisco. Despite that, Michael was enamored. All Joey had to do was sing, and Michael's frustrations would melt away.

Joey's birthday was on the horizon, and Michael had the perfect gift in mind. Riding his Vespa through the cold and foggy weather of San Francisco, Joey would often walk in the door soaked. His flimsy jacket, though fashionably bohemian, wasn't waterproof, and it had definitely seen better days. It was tattered, worn, and threadbare around the collar and elbows. Joey complained about the cold, jumping into a hot shower to warm up. He needed a riding jacket, and Michael had found a perfect fit at the mall in Daly City. Joey would never be caught dead shopping in the foggy suburb. But Michael had a nose for bargains and spotted a sale on outerwear.

Scanning the clothes rack, he was determined to find something practical yet sporty enough for Joey's eclectic fashion sense. It was not a simple task, but then he spotted it, a navy blue waterproof jacket. Michael tried it on and thought it would look good on Joey—it would accentuate his narrow waist and broaden his shoulders. The removable lining would allow him to wear it all year round, and the price was right. It was at the top end of Michael's budget. But Joey needed a good jacket, and Michael spared no expense.

The day arrived, and Michael couldn't wait to give him his

birthday gift. Joey had spent the day at the Zoo with a friend. Michael had tried to leave work early to give himself extra time to prepare, but there always seemed to be an eleventh-hour crisis. Michael was still busily preparing a special birthday dinner while Joey showered. He set the table, placed flowers in the center, and lit a candle. It was the perfect romantic setting. He pulled the large box from the closet and adjusted the bow on the wrapping. Placing it on Joey's chair, he could barely contain his excitement.

"What's this?" Joey asked as he shook his wet hair in Michael's direction. "Could this be a birthday present from my boyfriend?"

"Looks like it. Go ahead, open it."

Joey removed the bow and placed it around Michael's neck before unceremoniously tearing off the wrapping. Upon opening the box, his smiling face turned into a frown. Michael didn't understand his reaction.

"You've been complaining about how cold you are when driving your Vespa around town. I knew you needed something warmer. Try it on and see if it fits. Oh, and it's waterproof, so no more soaked clothes."

"It's very nice—yeah, it fits perfectly. Thank you."

"You seem disappointed. Don't you like it?"

"I do, yes. It's very practical."

"Practical? That's an odd way to describe it."

"Well, it is. I mean, I definitely needed a new jacket."

"But?"

"It's just that this is the sort of gift my mother would give me. Not something fun or playful."

Michael could feel his ire rising. He had put a lot of thought and money into this purchase. He had always put Joey's needs before his, and this was typical of his recent reactions.

"Fun or playful? Joey, I don't understand. You've been complaining about your tattered coat for months. I found something you genuinely need, but you'd rather have something else? What playful gift do you wish I got you?"

"I don't know. It's not that I'm ungrateful." Joey paused. "Like Trevor. He knows I like animals. He doesn't have much money these days, so he took me to the Zoo for my birthday. We just spent the day together

wandering from exhibit to exhibit. He was so sweet and considerate. I think it was the best gift I've ever received."

Michael's frustration simmered just below the surface. He walked to the kitchen and silently prepared the dinner plates. Joey seemed oblivious to his hurt feelings. During the meal, he continued chatting about his wonderful day. Michael cleared the dishes while Joey sat at the table, not lifting a finger as he watched Michael wash and put everything away. Michael couldn't hide his feelings any longer.

"Listen, Joey. I'm sorry that I disappointed you by tending to your practical needs. I'm sorry that the jacket wasn't fun enough for you or that the dinner I cooked for your birthday wasn't as special as the Zoo. I planned this for weeks and rushed home today to make everything perfect for you. Then all I hear about is Trevor and the perfect gift he gave you. Sometimes, I think we are on different planets."

"Hey, don't be such a drama queen," Joey said. "Maybe we are on different planets, but I do appreciate you. Sometimes I wish you'd let go—have a little more fun."

"You're right. I could use more fun. I'm just too busy paying the bills and keeping our lives together."

"There it is. It always comes down to money with you."

Michael had enough. He picked up Joey's new jacket and handed it to him.

"Time to go. Daddy's done taking care of you for the evening. Happy Birthday, Joey."

Joey let out a heavy sigh and walked out the door. Michael turned his head, gazing at the city lights shrouded in fog. *This really isn't working. I can't keep taking care of him only to have him throw it back in my face. I'm done.* Michael wearily laid his head on the pillow that night. He knew he had to break up with Joey. As much as he cared for him, Michael knew their worlds would never meet. They simply wanted different things in life.

CHAPTER SEVENTEEN
MOVING ON
1989

    The tension between Michael and Joey continued to intensify. The more successful Michael was in his work life, the more resentful Joey became.

    Roberta had recommended Michael for a position in the mayor's office. He never dreamed he would work so closely with the mayor. When the job came through, the celebrations never seemed to end. Michael was the toast of the town. Invited to fancy dinners and cocktail parties, he enjoyed every moment. He asked Joey to join him for a dinner party that included the mayor, and he reluctantly agreed. Michael pulled up in front of Joey's apartment and climbed the twenty steps to his door. Joey was still getting ready, so Michael sat on the sofa, checking his watch every ten seconds. He worried they'd be late for his first dinner with the mayor. When Joey finally came out of the shower, he wore his usual torn jeans and t-shirt.

    "You're not planning on wearing that to dinner, are you?"

    "Yeah, what's wrong with this?

    "It's the mayor, for god's sake. It's a formal event."

    "So I should wear a costume to impress a bunch of haughty

politicians? I don't think so," Joey said defiantly.

"It's at Fleur de Lys downtown. I'm pretty sure they require jackets."

"Then I'll put on a jacket. It would look fabulous with my jeans.

"Come on, Joey. This isn't funny. It's my first dinner with the mayor. I can't make a poor impression."

"You're embarrassed by how I dress, is that it? My, my, you've certainly become high and mighty since you've been working at city hall. Just remember, it was me who introduced you to Roberta. You would never have been hired if it wasn't for me."

"Oh, for fuck's sake, Joey. Who cares? Do you want me to lick your boots in supplication? Be forever in your debt? Your introduction may have gotten my foot in the door, but my hard work propelled me forward."

"Hardly. You're just another twink staffer they like to keep around. You know what? I have no desire to go to this dinner with you tonight. You're just as fake as those corrupt politicians. Have fun hobnobbing with the glitterati."

"You can't be serious. The mayor expects both of us to attend, and they've made reservations."

"Well, they can change them, can't they?"

"Dammit! You can't think of anyone else but yourself, can you? You don't even give a shit about how this will affect me."

"Oh now, don't go playing the woe-is-me card. You're just as selfish as I am. I'm just more honest about it," Joey replied.

"Fuck you, Joey! Stay home tonight and every night. I'm done making excuses for you," Michael yelled as he stormed out the door.

•••

Dinner at Fleur de Lys was an elegant affair. Michael had never been to a restaurant of that caliber. A line of white-gloved servers stood back from the table, ready to attend to the guests' every need. Not knowing the proper etiquette, Michael paused as each course was served, trying to figure out which utensils the others used, and then followed suit. They paired a perfect wine with each of the seven courses, and he was feeling no pain by the time they served the entrée. The alcohol freed

him from his inhibitions. So when Roberta asked why Joey hadn't come along, Michael gave her the entire story. He told it with such dramatic flair that most of the table stopped chatting and listened. Michael then launched into a description of life with Joey during that past year. They especially liked the vignette about Joey's birthday gift.

"Sounds like a real winner, Michael," one guest said.

"Joey is a nice guy," the supervisor added. "But he's certainly not the most ambitious person we know. To be honest, we never understood the attraction. You couldn't be more different."

"I don't know," Michael admitted. "I've always had a thing for lost causes. I'm always trying to fix things."

"The one thing I've learned from years of marriage," the mayor said, "is that you can't fix your spouse. As people grow older, they become more, not less. Love them as they are, or let them go."

Everyone at the table nodded in agreement, and the conversation turned to dating horror stories. Michael was relieved that he wasn't the only one with relationship issues. Each story emphasized some challenging element in a relationship, and he realized he had to do something about Joey. He wasn't happy. Their relationship wasn't working—it hadn't been working for months.

The following weekend, Michael and Joey met for lunch at the site of their first date. The Patio Cafe was buzzing with Castro clones—wearing the requisite 501 Levi jeans, T-shirt, and mustache. One of their favorite pastimes was to poke fun at the gay "uniform" and guess the stories of each couple in the restaurant—who was on their first date, who was the Daddy, who had been together way too long. They loved to make up stories about each table.

"What do you think they're saying about us today?" Joey asked.

"Well, we certainly don't give off that first-date vibe."

"No infatuated excitement at this table. So, what vibe are we giving?"

"You know the answer to that as well as I," Michael replied. "That scene Thursday night was the worst."

"It was. The only thing missing was a boxing ring. But look at us now—we're such adults, having a perfectly civilized conversation."

"That might be true, but there's something fundamentally wrong with our relationship, Joey. I can't take the drama anymore."

"Are you saying we're done—that you want to break up?"

"Yes. It's obvious that we want different things. It's not that I don't love you, Joey. You know that, right?"

"I guess I do. But if you love me, why can't we make this work?"

"Look, sometimes love is not enough. You will always resent my drive and ambition, and I will be frustrated by your complacency. We will continue disappointing each other."

Joey winced at his last comment and looked away. He scanned the other tables with a regretful look.

"I'm sorry it didn't work out between us," he said after a long pause.

"Me too. But I can honestly say that when I hear you sing, I will always feel a twinge of pain in my heart. You were my first boyfriend in San Francisco, and you'll always be special to me."

"I hope you find what you're looking for, Michael. You deserve to be happy."

The breakup was nothing like their constant fights. It was a relief. By acknowledging it wasn't working, they recognized what had initially brought them together. Although they'd continue to see each other at the gay men's chorus, Michael knew they could never be friends. Their values were completely different. He rested, knowing that they wouldn't be enemies either.

•••

I had to end my relationship with Joey, Michael thought. So why do I feel so sad? The breakup couldn't have gone any better. There was no yelling or gnashing of teeth—just a calm realization that they weren't right for one another. Despite that, Michael's heart ached. His friends at work took his side and supported him as best they could. Lourdes took him out to lunch each day during the weeks that followed. She told Michael that he was better off without Joey. Kenneth provided the distraction he needed. Barely a night went by that they didn't go two-stepping or to the Midnight Sun. His new friends were great, but Michael needed someone who truly knew him—someone with whom a

shared history lent a deeper understanding. Michael needed Ted.

It had been over a month since they had last spoken—a record. Michael poured himself a glass of wine, sat in his recliner, and dialed Ted's number. He half expected to get his answering machine, but instead, there was a recording:

This number is not in service. Please check to make sure you have the correct number and dial again.

He dialed two more times with the same result. Michael's heart beat rapidly. There was something wrong. He grabbed his phone book and looked up the number for Ted's sister. She answered on the first ring.

"Hi, Susan. It's Michael, Ted's friend from D.C. I've been trying to reach him, but his number is disconnected."

"Michael, I'm sorry I didn't call you. It's been insane here, as you can imagine."

"What do you mean? Is he with you?"

"Ted passed away two weeks ago."

"No, that's not possible. I just spoke to him last month. He was fine."

"It happened pretty quickly. Ted got pneumonia. His body was too weak to fight it. We're still in shock. I'm so sorry I didn't call you."

"He can't be gone. He's my best friend."

Michael choked on his words as grief tightened his throat. His eyes burned, and heat rose in his face. This can't be happening. It's just a bad dream. Michael hung up the phone and stared out at the twinkling lights of the San Francisco skyline. It wasn't the first of his friends to die of AIDS, but it was Ted. Somehow, all the memorials and funerals he attended over the past months came together in his mind. He gulped the rest of his wine and wept.

CHAPTER EIGHTEEN
FLEET WEEK
1991

Fleet Week in San Francisco always proved to be a good time. The city by the bay teemed with young sailors grateful for several hours of leave. A local journalist nicknamed San Francisco Baghdad by the Bay because of the array of colorful characters and cultures. Since the days of the gold rush, the city was known as a gathering place for all sorts. It's a town where nothing is truly out of place. If not accepting, San Francisco was certainly tolerant of diversity. The sixties brought the beat culture and hippies, and the seventies saw the dawn of gay liberation. Michael wasn't sure how the nineties would shape his new city, but he loved every aspect of his adopted home.

One of Fleet Week's pivotal events was the Blue Angels' air show. The Navy airmen would fly in formation over the entire city and bay. Red, white, and blue smoke colored the sky in their wake. The booming engines rumbled over every corner of the city. As an aide for a San Francisco supervisor, Michael had secured optimal tickets to the show. He accompanied Supervisor Achtenberg and her significant other to the viewing stands, receiving VIP treatment. He was beyond excited.

Michael was in his element among the other staffers and political

types. He could chat with anyone about anything. This job was a far cry from his counseling position at the high school in Virginia. Although he loved working with the kids, he had to be careful. It wasn't safe to be an out gay man in a public high school. If he suspected a student was struggling with their sexuality, Michael was careful not to reveal too much about himself. The last thing he needed was for rumors to start or, worse, to be accused of recruiting students to the "gay lifestyle."

His career in San Francisco couldn't have been more different. He worked for a lesbian city supervisor whose office actively wrote legislation protecting the rights of the gay community. Michael was right where he should have been—in the gay Mecca.

The Fleet Week air show did not disappoint. The formations were done with precision, and the stunts were frighteningly exciting. They entered the bay, flying over the Golden Gate Bridge on a bright, sunny October day. The sky was a brilliant blue backdrop to the red towers supporting the iconic suspension bridge. The crowd cheered with glee when the jets zoomed between the towers and into the bay. They flew over Alcatraz, around the Transamerica building, and Coit Tower from one end to another. Michael was filled with awe, mesmerized by their death-defying feats.

Almost as interesting as the air show were the people watching. Michael never tired of the colorful crowds attending the many events in San Francisco. The Folsom Street Fair, outdoor concerts, and Pride Month celebrations brought partiers from all over to express themselves in a city that accepted them without question. One of the best parts of Fleet Week was the throngs of sailors that invaded the city. He was titillated, watching their reactions to the colors of San Francisco on full display. A parade of men and women in uniform strolled by the viewing stand dressed in military whites. The image of Scott in Dupont Circle flashed in his mind. He was incredibly handsome, especially in his uniform. After all these years, Michael was struck by the glimmer of hope that Scott might be among the parade of sailors in the crowd. Perhaps he'd always be the one that got away. Michael was roused from his musings when he locked eyes with a familiar face.

"Michael? What are you doing in San Francisco?" Glen asked as

he pulled him into an unexpected bear hug.

"Glen, how many years has it been? You look as handsome as ever. Sorry, am I allowed to say that?"

"Hell, yes! In fact, you can call me hot chocolate!" He winked and flexed his muscles.

"Seriously!? You haven't changed a bit."

"The last I heard, you were at a school in Virginia. How did you end up in San Francisco?"

"That's right. I loved my job and the kids, of course. But I had to get out of that little town, if you know what I mean."

"Well, you certainly came to the right place. I come up here as often as possible, which is never enough."

"Up here? Where are you stationed?"

"San Diego. Just a few hours away. Been there for three years now."

"I'm surprised I haven't run into you in the Castro on one of your visits."

"Hey, I'd love to catch up. Do you have time for a drink?" Glen asked.

"Absolutely! Let's go to another neighborhood. We're in straightsville here."

Michael bid goodbye to the supervisor and his co-workers, who gave him mischievous looks when he introduced the handsome young officer. But he was careful not to take the bait. He would surely be ribbed mercilessly at work the following day. Then Glen and Michael walked to the parking garage and drove to the Castro.

•••

The historic Elephant Walk was a perfect place to spend the afternoon with its perfect view of the iconic gay neighborhood. The bar became famous after the assassinations of San Francisco Mayor Moscone and gay supervisor Harvey Milk. When Dan White was convicted of voluntary manslaughter rather than first-degree murder, all hell broke loose. His lawyers used what came to be called the Twinkie defense, saying that he was depressed and his overeating of junk foods was a symptom of his diminished mental capacity. The light sentence ignited protests that

ended with a riot and a police raid of the Elephant Walk. If there was any San Francisco monument to gay rights, it was the Elephant Walk. Ever since the riot, it has been a symbol of the fight for equal rights.

Still dressed in military whites, Glen turned many heads, especially in the Castro. His lack of prudence surprised Michael. What if he were seen in a gay bar? Wouldn't he be thrown out of the Navy? Seemingly, Glen didn't have a care in the world as he made a beeline to a window seat.

"This place is awesome, dude," Glen said. "I've never been here during the day. You can see all the boys from here."

"Sure enough, but don't you have to be careful not to be seen here?"

"If Clinton gets elected, no one will hunt for gays in the military. Things have gotten a lot easier lately."

"I wouldn't be so sure, Glen. Clinton is getting a lot of pushback for that campaign promise. Doing away with the ban on gays in the military isn't a slam dunk."

"Maybe not, but I think we're moving in the right direction. Enough about that, tell me about yourself. How do you like San Francisco?"

"I love it. Moving here has been the best decision I've ever made. I've only been here three years, but it feels like home."

"So, what about your love life? Are you with someone? Are you single? Tell me all."

"Are you trying to pick me up, Commander?"

"That's Captain if you please. And sure, why not? You're as cute as ever! Besides, what they say is true."

"What's that?"

Glen looked down and grabbed his crotch.

"Once you go Black, you never go back," Glen said as he wiggled his eyebrows.

"Oh my God, Glen. You pig, you're a piece of work!" Michael squealed and threw his napkin at him.

"So, what do you say, handsome? We're both single, and I'm on leave!"

"Dude, that'd be like sleeping with a brother," Michael said evasively.

"Now you've got the lingo. I am a brother, after all," Glen replied, and they roared with laughter.

Their afternoon together felt like old times—light and easy. Michael's heart swelled as he caught up with Glen. But there was one thing he wanted to know, and he was reluctant to ask. They danced around their years back in D.C., never mentioning Scott. Finally, Michael worked up his courage.

"Ah, I was wondering when he'd come up. Scott is doing great. He is still working at the hospital in D.C. He's a big deal these days."

"What do you mean?"

"He specialized in infectious diseases. He's one of the leading experts on HIV/AIDS."

"Holy shit. That's amazing," Michael said. He let out a heavy sigh. "This has been such a nightmare, and there's no end in sight. I've lost so many friends. Did you hear about Ted?"

"No! Please don't tell me he's sick."

"He died shortly after I moved here. I still can't believe he's gone."

"Shit, man. I loved that guy. We had so much fun together."

"You're being safe, aren't you, Glen?"

"Absolutely. With Dr. Scott on my back, I have no choice. You know, he's been hit hard."

"What do you mean? Is, is he sick?" Michael asked, fearing the answer.

"Not my story to tell, Michael. But he sees death every day of his life. You should call him."

"After all these years? I don't think so. We didn't end on good terms."

"Look, no one has ever loomed as large as you did. Don't you understand, Michael? You are his sun—his heart revolved around you—even after you left. I don't think he ever got over you."

"Get out of here, Glen. That was years ago, and we've both grown up since then."

"That's my point. You two are meant for each other. You were

both too young and self-centered to realize it back then. Call him," Glen said as he slid Scott's number across the table.

"Thanks, maybe I will."

"So, I suppose that's a negative on sleeping with me, then?" Glen asked.

"You never give up, do you?"

"Nope," Glen replied with a mischievous grin. "And it's served me quite well."

•••

Later that night, Michael sat in his apartment and stared at the business card Glen gave him. Seeing Scott's name scribbled on the back gave him butterflies. What is wrong with me? he wondered. What are these feelings about? If Scott had never gotten over Michael, could it also be true he had never gotten over Scott? So many thoughts swirled through his mind. He wondered if there was a deeper meaning to Glen's response regarding Scott's health. What did he mean by "Not my story to tell?" For a moment, he was worried about his health. Don't be fatalistic, Michael, he thought. I'm sure he's fine. Then he pictured Scott's smiling face looking back at him.

What the hell? he thought and dialed his number.

CHAPTER NINETEEN
THE VOICE MAIL
1989-1991

Scott was dead tired when he arrived at his quarters. His double shift was punctuated by losing another patient to AIDS. To so many of his colleagues, the numbers were statistics. But this was Scott's community. He built relationships of trust with these men, who were desperate for someone to give them hope. Desperate for someone to care about them, not keep them at a distance or treat them like lepers.

His colleagues warned him not to get emotionally involved with his patients. One of the first things they taught in med school was that professional distance is critical to effective treatment. But the AIDS ward was a battlefield. Young men, barely twenty years old, appeared with sores on their skin, strange cases of pneumonia, and other opportunistic infections. Some lingered for months, succumbing to one illness after another before passing away. Even more tragic were those who perished after only a week or two. Death and disease were all he had known since he started practicing medicine.

Scott stripped and flopped on the bed, only to be annoyed by the constant beep on his answering machine. A weary hand reached over and pressed play. He closed his eyes, fading into sleep when the voice

startled him awake.

"Hi, Scott, you'll never guess who this is. It's Michael. I ran into Glen today at the Fleet Week air show in San Francisco. We had a great time reliving our days in D.C. Anyway, he tells me you're doing great things regarding the AIDS epidemic. I'd love to catch up with you. Please call me when you get a chance."

Scott froze. Michael? Really? He rewound the tape and scribbled down his number. Should I call him? It's still early in San Francisco. Scott laid his head back on his pillow as images of their time together flashed in his memory. He had been head-over-heels in love with Michael. It had taken Scott years to get over him, if he ever did. How could I even consider opening up that wound again? He wondered if the call from Michael might be a sign. Perhaps there was a chance for them to get back together. NO! Don't do that to yourself.

Scott had been in a long-term relationship that had recently ended. Rick had not only broken Scott's heart but had betrayed his trust. Together for three years, they had been in a monogamous relationship. Although they couldn't live together, they shared an apartment whenever Scott could get away, and Rick was fine with keeping things on the down low. It never bothered him that Scott couldn't be out—he had himself a hot military man. Scott was strict about practicing safe sex. It was not worth gambling your life away for skin-to-skin contact. After two years together, however, he believed their commitment was secure enough to relax his practices.

"Rick, would you consider us married?"

"It certainly feels that way," Rick joked. "You drive me crazy with your anal-retentive cleaning and other quirks. What's it been now, two years? That's a record for gay relationships."

"It is, isn't it? Seriously, though, do you think it's time to make a commitment to each other?"

"I thought we already had, Scott. What are you getting at?"

"Since we're monogamous, and we love each other, perhaps it's time to stop using condoms. There is limited risk for those of us in committed relationships."

"Are you kidding? What did you do with my boyfriend? Where's

Dr. Scott?"

"Stop it. This is a serious conversation. If you agree, we should take this to the next level."

Rick let out a nervous laugh and shook his head. Scott didn't understand his hesitancy but pressed on.

"So, what do you say?"

"Yeah, sure. If that's what you want," Rick replied.

Scott scooped him up and carried him to their bedroom. For the first time in two years, they had sex without condoms. Scott felt free again, and their lovemaking was filled with newfound passion. That renewed passion sustained him through his horrific days and nights on the AIDS ward. No matter how heart-crushing it was to witness the darkness of that deadly disease, he believed he had a safe place at home with Rick.

But he didn't. Nearly a year later, Rick caught a cold he couldn't shake—it lasted months. Then, he developed a heavy cough and lost significant weight. Scott tried not to think the worst, but his experience told him a different story.

"Rick, have you been tested for HIV?"

"No, why? This is just a terrible cold. I'm fine."

"Let me listen to your chest," Scott ordered, placing his stethoscope on his back. "It sounds like pneumonia. I'm taking you to the hospital."

"No, I'm fine. Leave me alone," he shouted.

When Rick raised his voice, he fell into a coughing fit. Scott scooped him into his arms, wrapped a blanket around him, and placed him in the car. They did the usual battery of tests at the hospital, including X-rays and bloodwork. It took two weeks to get the results of his HIV test, but Scott already knew the diagnosis. For his own preservation, he kept himself at an emotional distance. Scott realized he needed to be tested for HIV as well. He asked one of his most trusted nurses to draw his blood.

"Please keep this between us, Martha."

"Scott, there's a good chance you'll be fine," she responded. "You can't give up hope."

She tried to reassure him, but Scott knew better. The odds were against him, and all he felt was an overwhelming sense of dread.

The following two weeks were torture. Each day, he reported to work and tended to his patients. Throughout the day, he checked on Rick, who was in surprisingly good spirits. His body was strong, and he fought off the pneumonia better than others on the ward. Scott was struck by his lack of gravity. *Doesn't he know that he's probably got AIDS? He can't be that oblivious.* Knowing Rick as he did, Scott didn't expect him to have a profound change of heart or a moment of clarity about how he had lived his life. Scott wondered if his playful, adorable mate was even capable of self-reflection. When he got the results of their bloodwork, Scott went numb. *How could I have let this happen?*

Although he was not his doctor, Scott wanted to be the one to deliver the news. He sat at Rick's bedside and took his hand. He wasn't angry. At least that was what he told himself. But he couldn't be. It had been his decision to stop practicing safe sex and trust Rick, however foolish it was. Yet, he still loved this man who had effectively put a target on his back. His internal conflict was so intense that he could hardly process the magnitude of their diagnosis. Scott took a step back from the turmoil within and took Rick's hand.

"You know what the results are, don't you?"

Rick nodded his head and looked away.

"Why? Why would you do this to us?"

"I... I don't know. I just didn't think it would happen to me."

"It didn't just happen to you. Because of you, it happened to me as well."

"So you blame me because you're HIV positive?"

"No, I blame myself for trusting you." The edge to his voice was unmistakable. "And what about fidelity? Did you feel any guilt about cheating on me? Do I mean that little to you?"

Rick turned his head and said nothing. What could he say? Scott's heart and mind flooded with admonitions. *Why the hell did they stop using condoms? He should have known better. How could Rick be so thoughtless? How long has he been cheating on me? Didn't he realize he wasn't just gambling with his own life but mine as well?* Question after

question shot through his mind. Angry, frustrated, and scared, Scott stared at an almost certain future. His own agonizing death, one that he witnessed every day at the hospital, flashed before his eyes. *How could I have let this happen?*

And yet there was love. Even after Rick's infidelity and betrayal, Scott still loved him. He promised to be there for him in whatever capacity he needed. He couldn't give in to his anger—if he did, he feared losing control. Thankfully, Rick moved out not long after his release from the hospital. When pressed for a reason, his response was simple.

"Scott, you always do what's right. But our relationship is broken. Every time you look at me, I can't help but believe you blame me for your HIV. I can't live with that."

Rick was right. Although he promised to care for him, Scott resented him. His anger simmered just below the surface—he couldn't even look him in the eye. In the ensuing months, Rick battled several more opportunistic infections. Less than a year later, he died. Two more of Scott's close friends became symptomatic during the following year. Scott spent every free evening nursing them back to health or getting them beyond their latest infection. After each illness, each agonizing death, one thought echoed in his mind. *I'm next. Who will be around to care for me when they're all gone?*

In the wake of such agony and grief, Michael's phone call came. He played his message repeatedly. His heart ached at hearing his voice, but he couldn't bring himself to return the call. Scott believed he was next. This was no time to reconnect with an old lover.

•••

The AIDS ward was in chaos. The trickle of young men coming in with pneumonia soon became a flood. So little was known about the disease in the early eighties. By the time Scott was in residency, they had understood it was transmitted through bodily fluids. However, convincing the gay community to use condoms or stop having sex was an impossible task. Pivotal events like the Stonewall riots and the San Francisco riots after the assassination of the first openly gay supervisor moved the cause to mainstream news. The gay liberation movement of the late seventies ushered in a new era of freedom. Once relegated to

back rooms of seedy bars, fearing the inevitable police raids and arrests, gay men shouted to be heard and seen. Demanding equal rights led to sexual freedom and expression. Sex became a symbol of their newfound political and social power. Any directive that curbed their sexual freedom looked and felt like oppression. Hadn't they just broken free of that?

The fear and denial that festered during the early years of the epidemic divided a newly unified community. Protests turned into pride parades and events—the festive celebrations marked how far they had come. They were their just rewards for the oppression they bore for years. But all that changed late in 1981 when over one hundred previously healthy gay men died from rare pneumonia. By June 1982, they called the newly discovered disease GRID Gay-Related Immune Deficiency. The medical community soon learned that it wasn't confined to gay men, but the label had done irreparable damage. By the time the term AIDS replaced GRID, gay men had become the enemy. Religious leaders deemed AIDS God's retribution for the depravity of homosexuals. Politicians called for the quarantine of gay men to prevent the spread to the larger population.

Before understanding how the disease was transmitted, scores of healthcare workers and first responders who feared for their lives refused to transport or treat AIDS patients. Ambulances even refused to pick up patients in gay neighborhoods. During his first years of residency, Scott witnessed the horror and devastation of his community unfold in his emergency room. One of the few who dived into caring for people with AIDS, he recognized far too many from his visits to Dupont Circle. The desperation of his patients led him to specialize in infectious diseases. He was determined to find a treatment to stop so many young people from dying.

This last year had been the worst yet. His two best friends, Brian and Roland, were his refuge throughout his residency. Renting a room in their house started as a place he could escape. If he met a guy on one of his rare nights off, he had somewhere to bring him. Over the years, they had become the best of friends. When Brian collapsed one evening, Roland's first call was to Scott. He was just finishing his shift at the hospital when he was called to the nurse's station.

"Call an ambulance, Roland. Get him here immediately. I'll be waiting for you at the entrance."

AIDS hit Brian hard. His pneumonia was followed by macular degeneration, and they stood by and watched the wasting syndrome eat away at his body. Every day after his shift at the hospital, Scott stopped by to see Brian and Roland. He often cooked dinner and sat with Brian until he fell asleep. Then Scott listened to Roland pour out his heart as he told of his fear of losing the love of his life. Physically and emotionally drained, Scott slipped into his own bed before he drifted off into a troubled sleep.

CHAPTER TWENTY
THE AIDS QUILT
1992

The AIDS Memorial Quilt had thousands of panels honoring so many people who had died since the beginning of the pandemic. The quilt had become so large that it was rarely shown in one place. But in October 1992, it was to be exhibited in its entirety on the National Mall in Washington, D.C. Everyone at San Francisco City Hall was talking about what an incredible event it would be. The impact of seeing the massive quilt blanketing the mall would be profound. What better way was there to show the impact of such loss on the world? No one had escaped the scourge—everybody Michael knew in San Francisco had lost friends or family to AIDS. In the office, Kenneth described how profound it was to see portions of the quilt displayed at Grace Cathedral. The other staffers were riveted by each personal story.

"We have to figure out a way to get to D.C. to see it," Kenneth said. "We need to mark this event."

"Hey, why don't we go together?" Lourdes proposed. "I've never seen my brother's panel with all the rest."

"Then we have to go. I'm sure we can work something out."

"I'd love to, but I just can't afford it," Michael responded.

"I hear that. There's got to be a way to cut costs. Do you guys have friends back there? Maybe we stay with someone you know?" Lourdes asked.

"Yeah, if we eliminate hotels, we can get one of those cheap flights," Kenneth agreed. "One of my buddies lives in Adams Morgan. Don't you have people there, Michael?"

"Yes, but we can't stay with him—long story. It's just such a huge chunk of change."

"The quilt won't be exhibited in its entirety ever again. There are too many panels," Kenneth reasoned. "We have to try."

"Look, if we each cut down on dinners and drinks, we can save enough money. What do you say?" Lourdes asked.

"I guess I'll be dining on refried beans and pasta for the next month," Michael complained.

"Nothing you haven't done before."

The three staffers were determined to make it happen. They promised to reevaluate their cash flow by the end of the month. But Michael was more impulsive. That night, he called the airline to check the cost of a flight. He was so excited when he discovered a non-refundable flight for less than $300. *What's one more expense on my credit card this month? It'll just blend in with my huge balance.*

Michael hung up the phone and couldn't contain his excitement. He had to tell someone. Then he thought back to his conversation with Glen nearly a year before when his feelings for Scott surfaced with a jolt. He called him that very night. *I wonder why Scott never called me back? If he never got over me, why didn't he respond?* Michael had an overwhelming desire to see him again. *To hell with it. Let me give it another try.*

Michael still had the business card on which Glen scribbled Scott's number buried in his wallet. He picked up the receiver and dialed.

"Hello, Captain Jameson speaking."

"Why, hello, Captain. This is a voice from your past."

"Michael?"

"You still recognize the sound of my voice. Very impressive."

"How could I ever forget your voice? You tortured me with it for

years."

"Nice, very nice," Michael said, laughing. "Is this how you greet me after all this time?"

"Absolutely, and you deserve every bit of torture I can give back." He paused. "It's good to hear from you."

"I wondered if you got my message a few months ago. When I didn't hear from you, I figured you didn't want to talk to me."

"It was a bad time, Michael. I had just lost a friend, and, well, I wasn't up for opening old wounds."

"I'm so sorry, Scott. We've both lost friends these last years."

"Too many."

"That's actually the reason for my call. I just booked a flight to D.C. to see the Names Quilt in October. I was hoping we could get together."

"Seriously? I'd love to see you. Do you have a place to stay?"

"Not yet, but I'll be traveling with some friends. I'm sure we'll figure something out."

An hour passed as if it were a minute. Falling into their banter, the two former lovers found themselves in familiar territory. Scott shared some of the darkness of his days in the AIDS ward. Michael told him of the many memorials at which he sang. The gravity of the years since they last spoke weighed on them both. Each told stories, reacted to current political events, and laughed at memories long forgotten. When Michael hung up the phone, his heart was full. He wasn't expecting the surge of affection welling up within him.

He caught his reflection, staring into nothingness with a silly smile. *What am I, sixteen years old? He has a life back there and is still in the Navy. There is no future for us.* Nevertheless, Michael longed for the days when they were together. Memories of happier times so many years ago blocked out the pain of loss.

CHAPTER TWENTY-ONE
ANTICIPATION
1992

"Hmmm, what was that all about?" Scott said aloud, his hand still resting on the telephone. He was struck by the wave of emotion washing over him and the profound desire to see Michael again despite the pain.

After the initial playful jabs, they had settled into their old comfortable rhythm. They had not been in touch for six or seven years, but he couldn't tell that from their animated conversation. They had both survived so much during their time apart. They dove right into the devastation AIDS had inflicted on their community of friends and shared their grief over cherished companions. Michael told him of his work with the city of San Francisco. Scott was impressed with the direction his life had taken. Michael had always been determined to effect positive change for the gay community, and he was doing just that. What surprised Scott was Michael's political savvy at city hall. He had channeled his desire to change the world into politics.

Scott described his experience as an infectious disease doctor during the AIDS crisis. He didn't feel the need to hold back as he described the constant loss and lack of hope in his daily life. He lamented

their inability to stop the spread of the disease or secure more funding from the government. Coming from different angles, both were part of something greater than themselves. Scott realized they had both grown up: they were less egocentric and more practical. Each was focused on making the world a better place. They were both hopeful that the 1992 presidential election would bring a positive change in the fight against AIDS and the acceptance of the gay community. After twelve years of Republican control and lack of funding, they were hungry for change.

"Here's the rub," Scott said. "For all the anti-gay rhetoric from the Republicans, most of the staffers aren't homophobic in person."

"What do you mean? Obviously, if they espouse legislation that limits funding for AIDS research and our rights, they are homophobic."

"The policies are, yes. But the individual staffers, and likely a few congressmen and senators, don't believe most of what their party says."

"How do you know?"

"Do you remember that gay bar in Adams Morgan, Badlands?"

"Of course. That's where all the professionals went after work."

"It's still pretty safe for me to go there and not blow my cover. Throughout this presidential campaign, I've seen scores of Republican staffers wearing red ties and silk scarves. They spend the day helping to write anti-gay speeches and policy, then hang out at the bars at night."

"But that's plainly hypocritical."

"Yes, it certainly is," Scott agreed. "It's also politics, as usual. That's why I'm glad to hear you're working within the system in San Francisco. You're really making a difference."

"I hope you're right. But it's an entirely different world out here on the west coast. I'm not sure I could ever live back east again. I've become quite accustomed to a progressive agenda and environment."

"Sounds like utopia, Michael."

"It kind of is. Maybe you can plan a trip out here for your next vacation."

"Great idea. Meanwhile, let's just pray that Clinton gets elected and we get some forward movement on the AIDS front."

•••

When Bill Clinton became president, Scott had great hopes that

he'd end the ban on gays in the military. Clinton was a loyal friend of the gay community and actively courted its vote during the campaign. For the first time in history, a president or candidate positively acknowledged them. Unfortunately, he got a great deal of pushback from Republicans and Democrats. Rather than eliminating the ban on gays, Clinton signed a bill into legislation called "Don't Ask, Don't Tell." It was meant to be a compromise. The military would no longer ask about sexual orientation. As long as individuals remained in the closet, they wouldn't be thrown out.

Clinton's policy spurred a backlash against LGBT people on both sides of the aisle. Thousands of service members continued to be discharged each year. There were even special military investigators who sought to trap sailors and soldiers by coming on to them. If the unsuspecting sailor took the bait, the military police would swoop in. The fear of being discovered and discharged was much worse than before. Scott became more paranoid, not going out to gay bars in Dupont Circle. Scott couldn't risk losing everything he'd worked so hard for.

The last time Scott saw Michael, he had been anxious about having the inevitable conversation about the military and their future together. This time, he was worried about having a much more dire conversation. *How can I tell him I'm HIV positive? I'm a doctor. I should have known better.*

What happened, happened—no use in picking at old wounds. Scott was content that he'd be able to see Michael one last time. He had so much to get off his chest. Scott fantasized about what it would have been like if he hadn't been so focused on his military career. He pictured himself getting an apartment with Michael and living their lives as Michael had always dreamed. If they had been together all these years, he wouldn't have contracted HIV. Life would have looked quite different. Scott shook his head. *Why dream about what might have been?* He had to live in the present—he didn't have the luxury of time. Life was literally too short.

Scott's military service was due to be renewed the following spring. Until now, he had simply assumed he would sign up for another stint. *What if I didn't? Perhaps I could live my final years without the*

fear of being discovered. I could finally live in peace as a gay man. The more he thought about it, the more secure he became in his resolve. He was a doctor, so he'd never have to worry about a job. Climbing the ladder in the Navy held little allure now that he was ill. What did his rank matter if he only had a couple more years to live?

Watching his friends die, he could see the fate that awaited him. Once he became symptomatic, the Navy would likely dig into his personal life. He could be dishonorably discharged when he needed his medical insurance the most. He couldn't bear the thought of that. It was time to come out.

CHAPTER TWENTY-TWO
REUNION
1992

At the end of August, Michael, Kenneth, and Lourdes met for lunch to decide whether they could afford the trip to D.C. for the quilt exhibition. Michael was beyond excited and couldn't wait to tell them he'd already purchased his ticket. He planned to be the last one to speak. But the conversation did not go the way he expected.

"This month has been a total disaster," Lourdes began. "The landlord raised my rent for the third year in a row. I can hardly afford it as it is."

"Tell me about it," Kenneth joined in. "My car broke down again. The garage said it'll cost $500 to repair it. And it's not like you can rely on MUNI. San Francisco has the worst public transit system."

"Wait, what are you guys saying? We're still planning to go to D.C., aren't we?"

"I don't see how I can afford it, Michael. I wish I could."

"I'm out too," Lourdes replied. "I'll have to see my brother's panel here in San Francisco."

"Good thing we haven't bought tickets yet. We would have been screwed," Kenneth said.

"Speak for yourself," Michael replied. "How could you guys abandon me like this?"

"What do you mean? We said we were going to reevaluate after we saved some cash."

"I just assumed we'd all make it work. When I found an incredible fare, I jumped at it. It's non-refundable."

"Dude, that sucks," said Kenneth.

"No, it doesn't," Lourdes argued. "You get to go to D.C. Who cares if we're not there with you? You'll be seeing all your old friends. You'll be just fine."

"I suppose you're right. But I was looking forward to showing you guys around."

That night, Michael dialed Scott's number once again. Now that he was traveling alone, he didn't feel comfortable asking to stay with Kenneth's friend in Adams Morgan. Most of Michael's friends left D.C. right after they finished their degrees, so he couldn't think of anywhere to stay. Michael hoped Scott might have some suggestions, and Scott did not disappoint him.

"Actually, a friend of mine has a house on Capitol Hill. I've rented a room from him and his lover for years. It's my private getaway."

"Do you think they'd mind having me there? I mean, they don't even know me."

"Oh, but they've known about you for years."

"Yikes, that doesn't sound good," Michael said. "What lies did you tell them?"

"Nothing but the truth, Michael. That you broke my heart and moved across the country to get away from me?"

"Hey, that's not fair. I wasn't trying to get away from you."

"Perhaps, but you broke my heart. But don't worry. I forgave you long ago."

"That was big of you," Michael said, trying to lighten things up.

"Seriously, you are welcome to stay there. Give me your flight information, and I'll pick you up."

"You're a lifesaver, Scott. Thank you."

Michael's flight was delayed getting into Dulles Airport. He hated Dulles—it was the most confusing airport he'd ever been to. One didn't board or deplane directly at the gate. They piled the passengers into a pod, transporting them to the plane or main terminal. When he finally got off the pod, he scanned the area for Scott. He was nowhere to be seen. He was sure they had changed the gate, and Scott was waiting for him somewhere in the terminal. Michael wondered if he should stay put so that Scott could find him or go looking for him. Michael knew the general rule was that one should stay put. Whoever you were meeting would probably come looking for you. If both parties wandered around, the likelihood of missing each other was greater. So Michael took a seat and scanned the terminal for Scott.

Thirty minutes passed, and Michael became increasingly anxious. *Maybe I should go to baggage claim. He's probably waiting for me there.* No luck: Scott wasn't there either. He figured it was the logical place to look and decided not to move. Surely, Scott would end up there.

•••

Scott waited eagerly at the gate. Michael's flight was over two hours late, and Scott was getting antsy. His pacing could have worn a groove in the carpet. When he checked with the attendant, she informed him that the flight was at a different gate. It was clear on the opposite side of the airport.

"You've got to be kidding me," Scott exclaimed. "Why wasn't there an announcement? I've been here for hours."

"I'm sure there was, sir. Sorry for the inconvenience."

Scott sprinted down the long corridor while glancing at the signs. In the distance, he could see no one at the gate. Out of breath, he leaned his hands on his knees and tried to catch his breath. *Now what?* He found another agent and asked about the flight.

"Oh, that flight came in approximately forty-five minutes ago. Have you checked baggage claim? I'm sure you'll find your friend there."

Exasperated, Scott made his way to baggage claim. He couldn't believe this was such a mess. *I hope he doesn't think I've forgotten about him. This is an auspicious way to begin our reunion,* he thought.

No sooner did the thought cross his mind than Michael's smiling

face appeared.

"Did you forget about me?"

"Are you kidding? I've been all over this godforsaken airport looking for you."

"I figured as much. This has been such a mess. I'm so sorry."

"Obviously, it's not your fault," Scott said, pulling Michael into a tight embrace. "Come on, let's get the hell out of here. I hate this airport."

It took most of the drive for their anxiety to wane. For all the comfort they derived from their phone conversations, Scott remained at an emotional distance. He couldn't let himself get swept away by Michael's charm. But damn, he looks better than he did seven years ago, he thought. He was happy for him. Michael deserved it.

Once at the house, Scott gave him the tour and introduced him to Roland.

"I thought you said you rented from a couple. Where's Roland's boyfriend?

"Brian died of AIDS last year, right around the time you first phoned me. It's the reason I didn't call you back. I was a mess and didn't have the emotional energy."

"Oh my God. I am so sorry, Scott. How's Roland doing?"

"As well as one can expect. I spend a lot of my free time with him these days."

"Good thing he has a friend like you in his life."

"It is. Anyway, let me show you to your room. Here, let me carry that. I'm sure you're eager to get some rest after that long, delayed flight," Scott said as he took his bags.

"Always so chivalrous, Scott. You've still got it, Captain."

"Do I, now? You better get your eyes checked, my friend. This workhorse has seen too many hard miles since we were together."

"The miles look good on you," Michael said with a wink.

"Here you go. There are fresh linens and towels. The bathroom is just down the hall and…"

Michael interrupted him with a kiss. Not just a peck on the lips but a deep, passionate kiss. Scott felt his body stiffen, but then he gave in

and let himself feel it again. I can't let this go any further without telling him about my HIV status, he thought. When Michael broke the kiss, he placed his hand under Scott's chin and looked into his eyes.

"Why did I ever let you go?"

"Oh, I don't know. Something about living a lie in the navy's closet."

"What a fool I was."

"Perhaps, Michael. But we both had a lot of growing up to do. I was so focused on my career that I didn't consider your feelings, at least not enough."

"Look, I didn't plan on bringing this up, especially since I just arrived. But honestly, I am overwhelmed by these emotions. Scott, I still have feelings for you."

"Let's slow down. We have the entire weekend to sort through all that. Can we just enjoy our reunion before getting too heavy?" Scott asked. He wasn't ready for that conversation.

"Aye, aye, Captain. Anything you say."

"You're a dick. You know that? And if I'm your commanding officer, you had better learn to follow my orders."

"Ooh, I like it when you get tough and manly."

"You had better behave, or I'll lock you in the brig."

Their laughter filled the house with much-needed warmth. They sat in the parlor and spent the rest of the evening reminiscing. As one glass of wine led to two and three, they filled in the details of their years apart. Each placed the missing pieces in their proper place, creating a puzzle depicting their lives. Each piece was a story that shaped the men they had become. Scott fought his desire to hold Michael in his arms once again. There was still one piece missing, but he wasn't ready to share it yet.

CHAPTER TWENTY-THREE
REALITY SETS IN
1992

 A sea of quilted panels washed over the National Mall, billowing waves of memorials as far as the eye could see. Three-by-six-foot glimpses into lives cut short by a senseless disease. Michael and Scott wandered down each aisle in solemn solidarity with the thousands who mourned and longed for what could have been. The sun shone brightly on that crisp October morning, but there was no levity in those gathered. Never had the mall been so quiet. Instead, it was filled with reverence and pain. Smiling faces appeared on panels; crafts or rainbows adorned others, symbolizing all the creative energy that no longer graced the earth. Each panel was a unique tribute to a vibrant person so well-loved.

 Michael carried the list of names and locations of their panels in his hands. Both he and Scott planned to visit their friends who had passed. But the sheer number laid out before them was overwhelming. No matter how great, numbers didn't have the impact of so many faces staring back at them. Passing so many by to get to those they knew seemed irreverent, as if they weren't honoring their own community. Row by row, they strolled through, and the hours passed. They had no sense of time. Then Michael stopped and held onto Scott for support.

Knees weak, he slumped to the ground. There it was—Ted's beautiful face smiling back at him.

"I had no idea, Michael. I'm so sorry."

"I didn't want to believe it myself," he began. "When Ted told me he had AIDS, I couldn't face it. We sat across from each other at our favorite diner, and he looked at me with sunken eyes, almost as if he were pleading with me to help him. I sat there, helpless, not knowing what to say."

"That's one of the worst parts of this goddamned disease," Scott added. "It snuffs the life out of them well before they die. Witnessing lively spirits and personalities get extinguished—it's even more painful than watching their physical decline. When they lose hope, it's like they've already died."

"You're so right. I never thought of it that way, but that is exactly how it feels. Then you're just waiting for their frail bodies to catch up to their broken hearts and minds."

They were silent for a bit. Michael kneeled before Ted's image, tears tracing down his cheeks. He reached out and touched the ebullient face, staring back at him. *Why did you have to die? You were too goddamn cute for your own good. Everyone wanted a piece of you.*

"I've lost so many, but this one…"

"This one won't stop hurting," Scott said, finishing his sentence. "He was your best friend. I don't think the pain of his loss will ever stop."

"Scott, I am so glad that you are with me for this. My friends in San Francisco didn't know him like you did, and I couldn't have done this alone."

"I'm not going anywhere, Michael. I am right here beside you."

Scott's heart broke once again. He knew he'd be following the same path someday soon. He helped Michael up, and they continued to walk. When they came upon Scott's friends, Michael asked him to share a bit about their lives. With each visit, they brought their loved ones into their midst with stories of their lives—laughter mixed with tears. The friends they had lost surrounded them. Scott put his arm around Michael, and they continued to the far end of the mall. Physically and emotionally spent, they had reached the end.

"Let's grab something to eat. We both need to get off our feet," Scott suggested.

"Can we go to Mr. Henry's for old time's sake? Is it still in business?"

"It sure is. The site of our first date; that's certainly appropriate."

Sitting down to dinner at their old haunt was precisely what they needed after the heavy afternoon on the mall. Michael's playfulness returned with animated descriptions of life at city hall. Scott wondered what it would be like to be with Michael again, and he could see that Michael was thinking the same thing. *I've got to stop this. There is no way I can be in a relationship now.*

But Scott couldn't help himself. He got a kick out of watching Michael bite into the colossal cheeseburger, ketchup dripping down his chin, lettuce falling out of the bun. Scott reached across the table, wiped the mess off Michael's chin, and brought it to his own mouth, licking it off his thumb. Then he winked.

"Ewwwwww! That is so gross."

"You think so? Maybe if you kept all the food in your mouth, I wouldn't have to clean you up."

"I can think of better ways for you to clean me up. Besides, there's nothing wrong with me enjoying my food," Michael said with mock indignation.

"Not at all. It seems you've worked up quite an appetite. You've always liked a fist full, or should I say, a mouth full of meat."

"Keep talking like that, and I'll devour you right in front of all these nice boys," Michael said as he swept his arm toward the dining room. "Then what would the navy do to you?"

"OK, OK, I give. Can't let them throw me out now. I've only got a few more months to go."

"What? Are you serious?"

"Yeah. I'm ready. It's been a great run, but it's time for me to live my own life. What's left of it," Scott admitted, saying that last phrase under his breath.

"Shit. I thought you'd be a career man until the very end. And what do you mean, what's left of it?"

"Nothing gets by you, does it, Michael? It's just that I realize how fleeting life can be. I mean, for years I have dedicated my life to helping all these dying men. Knowing that nothing I do will prevent them from dying has taken a toll on me. I'm surrounded by suffering and death every day. All I can do is hope to extend their lives and help them feel more comfortable. My career in the Navy doesn't seem to matter anymore. It's just not as important as living life to the fullest."

"But you are making a difference, Scott. I know you are. Thank God these people have someone like you who won't judge and who can be compassionate while treating their illness. What you're doing matters."

"I believe that's true. But I don't have to be in the Navy to be a good doctor. Can you imagine what it would be like for my patients to know that I'm gay, too? All the comfort they would take from that? I'm tired of living a lie. Walking through the virtual graveyard on the mall today only punctuated the need to act with integrity. I have to be open—free to be who I am as a gay man. I can't do that in the Navy."

"Wow! I never thought I'd see the day you said goodbye to the Navy. When your term is up, will you become a civilian?"

"I've already given notice. As of June first, I'll be a free man."

"I'm having a hard time wrapping my head around this, Scott. Being an officer was all you ever wanted—that and being a doctor. It just seems like there's more to it."

"There is. I promise to tell you. But I'm wiped out. Can we head back home and rest before the vigil tonight?"

•••

They curled up on Scott's bed and cuddled. The intensity of the emotions welling within startled Michael. Being with Scott felt like coming home. Michael's body fit comfortably against Scott as they spooned, his warm breath tickling Michael's ear. Dozing in and out of sleep, he imagined what their life might be like if they were to get back together. Would they live in D.C. like in the old days? Or maybe Scott would move to San Francisco and start anew? Michael pictured them taking walks, cooking dinner together, or traveling to Europe. The possibilities seemed endless. Scott's news today changed everything.

In his dreamy state, Michael pushed back into Scott, gently

writhing against his crotch. He could feel him getting hard, so he pushed harder. Michael turned his head and kissed Scott, flicking his tongue at his lips. Flipping over to face him, Michael moved his hands down to release him from the tight confines of his jeans. Scott gave into his ministrations and kissed him passionately. Michael broke the kiss and moved his head down to take Scott into his mouth. But Scott pulled back and lifted Michael back to face him.

"I think it's time we have a talk."

"Now? Why don't we finish what we're doing first? I don't want to lose my place," Michael said as he moved his head back down.

Scott sat up and took Michael's sweet face in his hands. He kissed him chastely on his lips and stood.

"You haven't changed a bit," Scott said, letting out a regretful laugh. "Why did I ever let you go?"

"I suppose we'll have to make up for all the time we lost," Michael said, reaching for Scott's zipper again.

"That may not be possible."

"Anything is possible, Scott."

"No, it's not. I don't know how to tell you this." Scott let out a heavy sigh. "It breaks my heart."

"Tell me what?"

"Michael, I'm HIV positive."

It was as if he had slapped him in the face. Michael was stunned into silence, but his heart and mind flooded with thoughts and emotions so jumbled he could hardly make sense of them. He could feel his face flush, and his eyes welled with tears.

"You? How? You're a doctor. How could that happen to you?" he said, shaking his head. He turned and paced the room, reeling from the news.

"Rick and I were in a monogamous relationship, so we stopped using condoms. He cheated on me. He'd been sleeping around a lot and, well..."

"What an asshole! How could he not practice safe sex when he knew he could infect you? That's just cruel."

"Rick wasn't cruel. It's just that he never thought of anyone but

himself. I'm sure it never even occurred to him that he might hurt me."

"That's so stupid. Everyone knows how HIV is spread. What the fuck!?"

"He was the king of denial," Scott said, looking away. "He could never face the consequences of his actions."

"How old was this guy? I mean, he sounds like an adolescent. I can't imagine how he could do this to you."

"He acted like a kid. Most of the time, it was endearing. But his reckless decisions destroyed both our lives. I have to take responsibility for my actions as well. We should have never stopped having safe sex. I wanted to believe our relationship was based on trust. I should have noticed the signs. Ultimately, I'm to blame for my choices. I should have known better."

"Are you kidding me, Scott? This guy doesn't protect himself while he cheats on you, then he deceives you, has unprotected sex with you, infects you, and you are blaming yourself? Come on!"

"I get your anger, Michael. It burned inside me—but I had to let it go. I had to forgive him. Otherwise, it would have eaten me alive."

Michael couldn't believe what he was hearing. How could this happen to Scott? He wanted to find Rick and curse at him. How could he do this to him? Lost in his anger and frustration, Michael noticed Scott sitting across the room, staring out the window. *What a selfish prick I am. I can't imagine what he's feeling right now.* He flew to him and sat on his knee.

"Hey, I'm sorry."

"Sorry for what?"

"For only thinking about myself. I can't imagine how betrayed you felt. You didn't deserve to be treated that way."

"Maybe not, but this is my reality now. It's also one of the main reasons I need to leave the Navy. I'm done with the lies. I have to live with integrity—for whatever time I have left."

"What are you saying—time you have left? You're not sick, are you? You take good care of yourself. Don't talk like that."

"I'm sorry, Michael. This is not the reunion you were hoping for. I couldn't let it go any further without telling you the truth. What we're

feeling for each other is simply not in the cards. But I'm so grateful to see you again."

"Listen, I don't know what I expected—obviously not this. But your life isn't over—and I want to be a part of it again."

"I'd like that, Michael. But I'm not sure either of us knows what that means." Scott turned to look out the window. He shook his head, and his eyes welled. "I have missed you so much."

Michael turned Scott's face and pulled it close to his. Gently, he kissed the tears streaming down Scott's face and pressed his lips against Scott's. They held on to each other for what seemed like hours.

CHAPTER TWENTY-FOUR
THE CANDLELIGHT VIGIL
1992

Dusk had settled on the mall with the amber glow of sunset lighting the western sky. Traces of the solemn day continued to blanket the gathering crowd. Michael and Scott approached the Lincoln Memorial steps along with thousands of others. As darkness won its battle over the light, flickering flames spread like stars across the reflecting pool. It glowed with the light of thousands of candles. It felt as if each soul extinguished by AIDS had come alive to join the throngs—as if their spirits returned to comfort the mourners.

Scott remained introspective after the intense discussion they had earlier that afternoon. A wave of relief washed over him. He was thankful that Michael didn't run right out the door. Although it shouldn't have surprised him, Michael's response was compassionate and tender. However, Scott feared that Michael would only feel anger and resentment toward Rick—that he wouldn't be able to get past the injustice of it all. But, when he sat in his lap and kissed him, Scott knew it would be all right. His friend was back. Friend: that was all he could be. Scott convinced himself that it was best for both of them. He couldn't put Michael through the inevitable death of a lover.

And yet here they were, holding hands at the vigil. Listening to one inspiring speaker after another, they clung to each other. The organizers led them in songs and prayers. As Scott scanned the crowd, he saw many men in far worse shape than himself. They all knew what lay ahead—their fates were all but sealed. And as moving as it was, one thought swirled in his mind: I'm next, and I don't know how much longer do I have?

Liza Minnelli took to the podium and slapped him out of his self-pity. The crowd went wild with adoration for this gay icon. Everyone hoped for a rousing speech or a song to lift their spirits. Instead, Minnelli rambled on, hardly making sense. Disparate phrases haphazardly strung together hung in the air. Her thoughts were so disorganized that she lost her thread. Finally, she asked the crowd to join her in the Lord's Prayer. Michael turned to Scott with surprise.

"How could she lead us in a Christian prayer? There must be many beliefs here—it excludes so many. This would never happen in San Francisco."

"I couldn't agree more. She must be drunk or on something. Nothing she's said made any sense."

"Well, people seem to be more amused than offended. That's good, right?" Michael quipped.

Thankfully, those who spoke after her brought the ceremony back into focus. When it was over, Michael leaned in and kissed Scott on the lips. He took his hand and turned.

"Let's take a walk."

"Don't you think we've been on our feet enough today?" Scott asked.

"Maybe. But there's nothing like D.C. at night. I'd forgotten how beautiful it looked with all the monuments lit up. Plus, I'm not ready to let go of this feeling."

"I know what you mean. Other than Liza, the vigil was incredibly moving."

Comfortable in the silence, they walked hand in hand, watching clusters of people sharing their emotions. A chilly breeze nipped at them as they strolled.

"So, I've been thinking," Michael began.

"Uh, oh. That always spells trouble."

"Hear me out. When you pulled away from me this afternoon, it was like you were afraid I'd get infected."

"That's true. But it was also because I needed you to know my status before we did anything. You needed to understand the risks."

"That makes perfect sense. But shouldn't we always approach sex as if one's partner is positive? Shouldn't we practice safe sex, no matter what?"

"You certainly know the facts. You're right. As is evidenced by my unfortunate situation with Rick, we must always protect ourselves. Always."

"Right. So, there is nothing dangerous about you and I having sex, is there?"

"Well, there is always a risk, Michael. You know that. It should be called safer sex, not safe sex. There is always the possibility of something going wrong."

"I understand that. But those are calculated risks, and the possibility of infection is extremely low. Isn't that right?"

"Right again. What are you getting at, Michael?"

"Look, it's obvious that we are picking up where we left off. Neither of us has been very good at hiding our resurgent feelings, and it is clear that it's not just lust. That being said, I want to have sex with you."

"Man, you're blunt. Yes, but we must be careful of our hearts and health."

Scott had to say it. He didn't want to hurt Michael. But deep down, he didn't want to get his own heartbroken again. Michael would leave in two days, and now he would be thousands of miles away. Scott couldn't simply hop in a car and drive a few hours to see him. Scott resolved to be vigilant with his feelings. He had to take care of himself. *I'm not as strong as I used to be.*

•••

They rested the following day. They were physically and emotionally drained. Their conversations were filled with anxiety, fear,

and uncertainty. Scott and Michael had spent hours filling in their recent history—where they had been and what they had experienced since they were apart. Michael wasn't sure if their reignited feelings would go anywhere, but he had no intention of holding back. Lovemaking the night before had been pretty tame. They were exhausted from the long day. However, Michael had no intention of holding back today.

After brunch, they returned to Scott's room, rolling around on his bed. They giggled like teenagers making out, tickling each other, and dozing off. Michael and Scott were entirely comfortable with each other's bodies. Scott's washboard abs were more cut than he remembered them to be. He ran his fingers over each bump and into the groves between his chiseled muscles. Nothing turned him on more than rippling abs—that and bulging biceps. *How did I get so lucky? Most guys just fantasize about being with a body like Scott's.*

Soon, he had peeled off Scott's briefs. He was as hard as a rock, and Michael wanted him inside him. He reached over to the nightstand to grab a condom when Scott intercepted him.

"Here, let me."

Michael expected him to place it on himself. Instead, Scott flipped Michael onto his back and rolled the condom onto him.

"What are you doing?" Michael asked.

"I think you know. I want you to top."

"But we've never…"

"Right. So isn't this exciting and new?" Scott said as he took them in a new direction.

Michael's eyes nearly rolled into his head, engulfed by his heat. Soon, he was lost in their shared passion—a first for him. Although he surmised Scott did not want to risk being on top for fear of infecting Michael, he made a mental note to have that discussion when they had clearer heads. For the moment, he let himself be swept away by an unexpected experience.

"Well, what do you know? You can be butch if you try," Scott said after catching his breath.

"Fuck you! I've always been butch, just not a top."

"So, what did you think? Did you like it?"

"What do you think? Honestly, anything we do when making love feels right. I'd forgotten how right it feels to be with you."

"To be honest," Scott confessed, "I've never forgotten."

CHAPTER TWENTY-FIVE
SEPARATION—AGAIN
1992

During the last three days, Michael was hit with one surprise after another. What had begun as a solemn pilgrimage to honor people who had died of AIDS had developed into a life-changing reunion. Being honest with himself, Michael knew his connection to Scott had never disappeared entirely. Although he had moved on with his life, Michael always wondered if he had made a mistake. Had he let go of his one true love? It was silly to hang on to an image of his knight in shining armor, but he couldn't deny the overwhelming feeling of love for this man he left years ago. The navy had always been the chief obstacle in their relationship—his retirement changed everything.

Scott's sobering revelation about his HIV status threw him into an emotional tailspin. He was angry at Rick for lying, cheating, and infecting Scott. He was heartbroken at the thought of Scott becoming symptomatic, suffering, and dying. Yet, he wanted nothing more than to be with him and love him. He didn't think twice about making love with him.

Now, he sat across from Scott at the airport, waiting for his flight to take him three thousand miles away. *What happens now? I live on the*

opposite side of the country. I have a job I love and friends who have become family. Am I willing to let all that go? None of it made any sense. He shook his head and chose not to think about it. This thing with Scott was way too complicated.

Scott reached across the table and pulled Michael's hands toward him.

"Hey, where'd you go?" he asked. "You haven't even left yet, and you're thousands of miles away."

"I don't know. Just thinking."

"Obviously. Are you OK?"

"Yeah, of course," Michael replied. "It's just that so much has happened this weekend. I'm not really sure how to process all this."

"You mean us?"

"Yes, with us, with you, with me. I felt blindsided so many times over the last three days. There's a lot to sort out."

"That makes sense," Scott said. "So much to take in. And what about us? Where do we go from here?"

There was the question Michael was afraid to answer. In truth, he didn't know. There was nothing practical about starting a relationship with a guy living thousands of miles away. Then, there was the fact that he was HIV positive. It would not make a vast difference to him, but it certainly complicated matters. Perhaps they were just being too impulsive. For once, Michael thought he shouldn't throw himself before the oncoming train. He was at a complete loss.

"Let's just see what happens, OK?" Michael said, then lowered his eyes.

Scott lifted Michael's chin gently. "Hey, I know you've had a lot thrown at you this weekend. All I ask is that you hear me out." His voice was filled with tenderness. "I have a very different perspective these days. I don't know what the future will bring, but I do know that life rarely gives us a second chance. And here we are, with an opportunity before us. I'm not ready to throw my second chance with you away."

Michael, rarely at a loss for words, said nothing as his eyes welled up and tears trickled down his face. In his heart, he knew he couldn't let their second chance pass. There was only one right choice: He and Scott

were meant to be together.

⋯

They had a tearful goodbye at the gate, and then Michael robotically walked down the narrow aisle to his seat. He was numb as he buckled the seatbelt and settled in for a six-hour flight. What am I going to do? he wondered.

He opened his journal and, through his tears, Michael put his pen to the page: What the hell just happened? Last week, I was perfectly content with my life in San Francisco. My buddies at city hall were my confidants and best friends. Working with the city supervisors and the mayor's office was thrilling. It's the best job I've ever had. No, I don't have a boyfriend anymore. So what if I broke up with Joey? It was a dead-end relationship with a guy who couldn't pay his bills. I was a sucker for way too long. It has been so much fun playing the field as a single man in San Francisco this last year. Why couldn't I fall in love with someone local? Why Scott? Why now?

Michael looked up when the flight attendant came by with drinks. He wasn't aware of the tears staining his cheeks.

"Oh my," the attendant said. "It looks like someone needs a stiff drink."

"That's the best offer I've had today," Michael responded, playing along.

Michael tried to sort out his conflicting emotions. None of it made any sense. Back at the airport, he was perfectly content with his solution to let things unfold naturally. And while he knew he was just avoiding the issue, it served his purposes well enough. Then Captain Scott had to ruin it all. He was always the one who was reserved—constantly making fun of Michael's sentimental responses. But not this time. Scott's words rang in his head, repeatedly making him tear up. "I'm not ready to throw my second chance with you away." How could he resist that?

CHAPTER TWENTY-SIX
BACK TOGETHER
1992

Michael and Scott spoke on the phone every night after his trip to D.C. They chatted as if they were together after a long day at work. They lamented the vast distance between them. Plotting and planning, they imagined what they'd do on their next visit. Scott mentioned he had accrued several days for leave. They had to be used before he retired, so he suggested a visit.

"Why don't you come for Thanksgiving? I have both Thursday and Friday off. I invited a few friends over for a traditional holiday dinner."

"Actually, I've already booked my flight. I could have surprised you if you weren't so assertive," Scott teased.

"No way! I'm so psyched!" Michael paused. "Wait, do you mean aggressive?"

"I said assertive, not aggressive, and it's not a criticism, Michael. Somehow, you make your desires known. More often than not, you get your way."

"Is that bad? Is it selfish?" Michael became immediately insecure.

"It's not bad at all, my love. Most of us dance around, afraid to say what we want. Then, we get resentful when things don't go our way. At least I never have to guess with you."

"It's just that I don't want you to feel like it's always about me."

"But isn't it all about you?" Scott said, teasing Michael.

"Now you're making me paranoid. Am I selfish, Scott?"

"No. You're sweet and generous and adorable."

"Promise you'll tell me if I'm being a jerk. I want you to feel heard."

"Oh, don't worry about that! I'm happy to point out your flaws."

"Hm, I'm not sure I won this point. Anyway, when will you arrive?"

"I'll get there Wednesday afternoon. We'll have five full days together."

Michael had everything planned by the day of Scott's arrival. He invited Lourdes and Kenneth from city hall along with their significant others. He asked them to bring a side dish. Then he stopped at the Safeway to buy the turkey. Michael wasn't sure what size he should get for six people. He loved leftovers, so he chose the largest bird he could find. The nineteen-pound turkey barely fit into his cart. Having chosen the main course for dinner, he turned his attention to the sides. He found a recipe for homemade stuffing and searched the aisles for the ingredients: white bread, walnuts, celery. Then he spotted the box of stovetop stuffing. That was it. Why bother making it from scratch when it was all done for you? He plopped it in his cart, and he was on his way.

Before long, it was time to get Scott from the airport. Michael's tiny Honda Civic was on its last leg, but it got him where he needed to go. On the way, Michael picked up a bouquet of roses. He paused as he handed over his credit card. Is this too much? Am I moving too fast? He let his worries pass and raced to the gate with flowers in hand. Michael wanted to greet Scott as he deplaned. He made a sign decorated with rainbows and hearts saying, Welcome to San Francisco, Captain Scott! He hoped Scott would get a kick out of it. One by one, the passengers came down the companionway greeted by boyfriends, girlfriends, and family members. Men kissed men, and women kissed women. No one batted an eye at same-sex couples. It was the reason Michael felt at home in San Francisco. Gay people were a normal part of life here.

When he spotted Scott nearing the exit, Michael held up his sign and yelled, Welcome home!

"Seriously, Michael. Could you be more melodramatic?" Scott said as Michael engulfed him in a hearty embrace.

"You know you love it, Captain." Then he kissed him right on the lips.

"Dude, enough with the captain shit. I still have a few months left. Let's not tempt fate."

"Good point. Come on, let's get you out of here. Are you hungry?"

"Famished. Airplane food is the worst."

"Since we'll be cooking all day tomorrow, I thought we'd grab a

pizza at the Sausage Factory in the Castro."

"Sausage Factory? Are you sure all they serve is pizza?"

"Well, anything else is extra."

"There's only one sausage I'm interested in. Let's stick with the pizza."

"Good answer. Let's go."

•••

Scott looked at the enormous bird in Michael's fridge. It took up the entire top shelf. Opening the fruit and vegetable drawers, he discovered they were empty. He wondered where all the food was. Surely, this can't be everything.

"You're up early," a sleepy-eyed Michael croaked as he entered the kitchen.

"I brewed coffee—nice and strong, the way you like it," Scott said, kissing him on the head.

"You're the best. I could get used to this."

"Hey, where's all the food for today? All I see is the giant turkey."

"The others are bringing the side dishes. All we have to cook is the turkey and stuffing," Michael responded, sipping his coffee.

"But there's no bread or vegetables for the stuffing."

"Look in the cabinet to your right." Michael was not used to speaking until after his first cup of coffee. Scott knew their conversation was pure torture.

"Stove Top stuffing? Don't take this the wrong way, but that's garbage."

"Is it? I've never had it before."

"Do you know what the others are bringing? We should make sure we have a balanced meal."

"I'm sure whatever they bring will be fine, but I could ask."

"Can I make a suggestion? Why don't I run to the market and pick up some stuff? I haven't cooked in ages, and Thanksgiving is one of my favorite holidays. I'd love to prepare some of my mom's traditional dishes."

"Go crazy, Scott. Honestly, I haven't the slightest idea how to cook a turkey. I would be grateful for the help."

"That's good because roasting that thing will take all day. We had better get started now, or it won't be ready in time for dinner."

"Really? OK, chef, I'm at your service. Put me to work."

Scott was relieved that Michael didn't take offense at his offer to cook. But he was surprised by how little preparation Michael had done. Scott returned from Safeway with potatoes, celery, carrots, green beans, and bags of other ingredients. He didn't know what the others were bringing, but he was sure it would be awful. Scott acknowledged he was a control freak, and Michael knew that from their years together. He happily sat by Scott, peeling potatoes, cutting green beans, and slicing carrots. Scott smiled at the domestic scene they painted as they prepared their first Thanksgiving meal together.

By the time the guests arrived, Scott had laid out a feast. None of them could believe their eyes. Michael proudly bragged that it was all Scott's doing. Scott wore a silly grin, watching Michael showing off his old boyfriend to his San Francisco friends. He felt he had passed the first test of fitting into Michael's world. It had been years since Scott felt at home—with Michael and himself. Could he dare to hope once again? Could Michael and I have a future together?

CHAPTER TWENTY-SEVEN
DESPITE IT ALL
1992

    Michael may not have been the best at getting Thanksgiving dinner together. Still, he planned every moment of Scott's visit to his beloved city. Michael was so proud of San Francisco and wanted Scott to fall in love with it, too. Their first stop was a tour of city hall. They entered from the main doors facing the Civic Center Plaza. Michael stood aside to watch Scott's reaction to the grand staircase that proudly graced the center hall. He recounted the local history, including the tragic assassination of Mayor Moscone and Harvey Milk. Very few people worked over the holiday weekend, so Michael brought him to the mayor's and the supervisor's chambers.

    Afterward, they visited the historic Mission Dolores, the first building in the City of San Francisco, in 1776. Behind the mission, they wandered through the only graveyard in the city. He showed Scott the notable people buried there: the first Mexican governor of Alta California, Luis Arguello, members of the Noe family, and other names that appeared all over the city in some form. The sun was shining, so they hiked up the hill to Dolores beach—an area of Dolores Park where all the gay boys sunned themselves on blankets as they cruised each other.

The view from the hilltop was stunning—all of downtown and the Bay Bridge were laid out before them.

What struck Michael most about their time together was how much they felt and acted like a couple again. They spoke about things they wanted to do and dreamed about places to travel. It was as if they were planning their lives together. They didn't dwell on the details or the fact that they were living thousands of miles from one another. Dreams became real in their imagination.

"Once I've retired from the Navy, I can travel anywhere I like. We could go to Europe or Asia—take a real vacation."

"God, I would love that. I've always wanted to visit Ireland and Spain."

"We could do that, you know. I'll be all yours in a few short months."

"All mine. Damn, that sounds good. If you could live anywhere in the country, where would it be?"

"Now that's a pointed question. I love D.C. You know that. But I think I'm done there. These last few years have been filled with sadness—so much death."

"Yeah, you've been in the thick of it."

"To answer your question, I suppose San Francisco would be an amazing place to live. You've certainly done a great job selling it to me… Could that have been your intention?"

"Maaaaaybe," Michael said with a sly grin. "Couldn't you picture yourself here with me? We could get a bigger apartment—maybe something in the Castro."

"We may be getting ahead of ourselves here," Scott replied, inserting a bit of reality into the conversation. "Let's take one step at a time."

"I suppose you're right. But I don't want us to waste any time, Scott."

They both knew the meaning behind his statement. Who knew how much time they had left together?

•••

On Sunday evening, reality struck him all at once. Scott sat

crouched on the floor in the center of the room. The already cramped studio apartment closed in around him, making him feel even smaller. He convulsed as his body trembled and tears poured from his eyes. Rocking back and forth, he sobbed, crying with abandon. It was as if months and months, years and years of pain and grief, had found their outlet. And once he turned on the spigot, there was no stopping the tears. He wept for his dead friend Brian; he wept for his dead friend Robert; he cried for the countless men who wasted away before their lives had even begun. He cried for the men, in the prime of their lives—brimming with youth, living life to its fullest—who suffered agonizing deaths. These men were struck by a disease that crept into their bodies simply because they expressed their love or dared to have sex with another man. AIDS attacked every healthy cell. One day, they were healthy; the next, they lay dying—dark purple sores appearing hidden under an arm or the inside of the leg, spreading to the neck and arms and faces.

Scott cried because he knew his fate. He was on borrowed time. Why then should he find love now when it was all going to end—when it would all come crashing down upon him? His body, his mind, and his heart could be crushed at any moment. Scott knew he was next; he knew it, even though he couldn't feel anything yet. His body was breaking down. He had watched and cared for his entire group of friends as they turned from healthy, strong, and virile men to wisps of fragile bones—with skin hanging loose from their limbs.

The years he spent in the AIDS ward during his residency were draining enough, but taking care of his own friends was overwhelming. Each of those men reached out to him, fell in love with him, and sought him out. Scott was one of the few people who would dare to touch, caress, and care for them in their last moments. Yes, Scott knew he was next. And here was Michael, who had returned to his life after so many years—healthy, loving, and beautiful. He felt Michael's muscular arms engulf his trembling body, and he continued to sob. How could this be? Why had they found each other again after so many years, just for him to die before they could even begin their lives together?

Scott's anger mingled with his grief. No, he didn't want to die. At last, there was someone to live for. Scott had long ago accepted his

fate. He understood it better every time he changed soaked bed linens or prepared meals that would never be eaten—every time he cleaned shit off the bathroom floor and wiped his friend's boney ass after an accident. Scott was diligent and methodical in his care. He had done this for several of his dearest friends already. As a doctor, smells and unfortunate bodily functions did not gross him out. They were the manifestation of the ugliness of a disease that wracked the bodies of these beautiful young men. Scott never even thought to run from the putrid stench of rotting flesh, a mouth filled with thrush, breath that belied the decaying cells within. He knew the wretched virus flourished as it made its onslaught throughout his own fragile body. Although Scott seemed the image of masculine virility, he understood the enemy was lying in wait. It was only a matter of time until it reared its ugliness and became known.

Scott feared his future with every friend who fell from the plague—a plague that ravaged the world around him. Who will be left to take care of me? Now, after seven years apart, Michael had entered his life again. Scott felt his heart ripping apart, aching for what might be while knowing the torture he would inevitably inflict on him. Scott couldn't allow that to happen. He would not subject the only man he had ever truly loved to unspeakable pain and loss. But what about me? Surely, I deserve to be loved, to have someone care for me—someone to comfort me. Scott's tears fell, in part, because he refused to let Michael go through such agony. He couldn't subject him to the fate of caring for a dying man. But then there was his abject need—Scott was powerless. His heart ached for Michael. Never had he wanted anyone so badly. How could he turn away from love when he required it most? Scott was trapped by his fear and his need.

Neither of them spoke throughout his raw display of agony. Scott knew that his profound vulnerability shocked Michael and probably broke his heart. But he could no longer hold back—he had to let go. Michael always let his feelings out, expressing frustration and anger or joy with exuberance. However, Scott could almost feel Michael's resolve to remain steady as Scott melted into his tears. He felt Michael's strength emanating from his tight embrace. It was a role reversal of sorts. Scott was used to being the caretaker. But having Michael minister to his needs

tasted like honey, soothing his parched throat.

The tears melted into resignation. Scott steadied his breath, trying to calm his burning thoughts. Letting go of his need to control, Scott rested, knowing that Michael was his heart. Whatever fate awaited them, they would do it together.

"I'm sorry, Michael. None of this makes any sense."

"Don't... don't apologize."

"What are we doing here, Michael?"

"What do you mean? We love each other, so we are following our hearts."

"You know, it's not as simple as that. I have it, just like Roland and Brian—just like Ted and so many friends we've lost."

"Scott, I love you and need to be with you. We'll face whatever happens together."

"That's my point. I don't know how much time I have left. I may look healthy to you, but my T-cell count is nonexistent. How can I put you through that?"

"I love you, and that is not your choice to make. It's mine. Cutting you out of my life would be like carving the heart out of my chest. I can't simply choose not to love you. Don't you understand that? I don't care if I only have you for a year, two years, or whatever. I want you for as long as I can have you. For me, there is no other choice."

"I love you too, but we both know what lies ahead, and it's not pretty. How can you sign on for inevitable torture?"

"I'm not signing on for torture. I'm signing on for a life with the man who rocked my world so many years ago and still does today—for the man whose love I cannot live without. Don't you see? I look at our lives together, however short, and look forward to each intimate moment—morning coffee, napping on the couch, walks on the beach. The darkness may inevitably come, but I choose to embrace every bit of the light that you have brought into my life. Scott, we can't throw this away for fear of what we might lose. Let's hold on to it and cherish every moment we will gain. I'm signing on for every moment I can get with you."

Scott looked into Michael's eyes with disbelief and gratitude.

How is this possible? I don't deserve this. But God knows I need him more than ever. He turned his head, and Michael moved to look at him directly. Scott sank into his brown eyes and thanked God for bringing Michael back into his life. His heart was bursting with inexplicable joy, mingled with the dread that their time together would be tainted all too soon.

•••

Michael kneeled on the floor behind Scott. He wrapped his hands around him and rested his face against the back of his head. Michael, never at a loss for words, was strangely mute during Scott's emotional break. He didn't know what lay ahead—how much time he would have with Scott. But Michael was confident of one thing—he would never let him go. When Michael learned Scott was HIV positive, he felt a steely grip on his heart. He felt as if it was he himself who was ill. Although he had kept up with Scott through mutual friends, they hadn't spoken in years. They had both moved on with their lives. They had to. But Michael never stopped loving Scott. He wondered if they would have stayed together if not for Scott's military career.

And now they were at a crossroads once again. Neither could have predicted the outcome of that fateful trip to D.C. They both had happy, full lives—at least, that's what Michael had thought. Despite the devastating news of Scott's health, Michael felt more strongly toward him than he ever had. The depth of his love for Scott frightened him. Michael knew what everyone would say. "How could you fall in love with someone who is HIV positive? Are you crazy? What if you get infected?" Perhaps he had those same thoughts. He was afraid for his own health. But he believed that safe sex worked. What Michael feared the most was losing Scott. After all these years apart, they had finally found each other. It was a cruel twist of fate—not just for Scott, but for Michael. Holding Scott in his arms that night, there was no other choice. His heart wouldn't let him give up on Scott—not now, not ever. He would celebrate every single moment with the man he loved, even if their life together was to be inhumanely short. Michael understood there was no decision to be made. Scott was his destiny, and he would cherish however much time they had left. Scott was his life now.

CHAPTER TWENTY-EIGHT
CHRISTMAS
1992

Michael couldn't wait to get back east. He hadn't been home for Christmas in years. He missed his family and the traditions he cherished. Although he didn't attend regularly, he envisioned his parish church decorated for midnight mass. Michael wondered if the church choir was still as good as when he sang with it as a kid; he remembered having a crush on the director.

He was hoping they could attend Mass as a family. But this year would be different. This year, he was bringing a man home to meet his parents.

Michael recalled the strife he experienced when he came out to them. It was during his first trip back to Virginia after having moved to San Francisco. His parents didn't understand why he would leave his friends and family to move thousands of miles away. Whenever he called home, his mother would ask when he was returning.

On that visit, after a year in San Francisco, his mother asked Michael when he was coming home for good.

"When are you going to stop this foolishness and move back? I know you like it there, but it's too far away."

"Mom, it's not that I enjoy being far from you and the family."

"Then come home," she interrupted. "You can live here until you find a job. I'm sure North Cross would take you back in a second."

"I can't do that, Mom."

"Why not? We're your family. You should be close by. Isn't that right, Eric?"

"Your mother is right, son. We just don't understand why you got up and moved. You had a good job, and you were happy. It makes no sense."

Michael hadn't intended to come out on that trip, but here was the opportunity. He took a deep breath and blurted it out.

"I moved to San Francisco because I'm gay. I needed to live where I didn't feel like an alien—where I could find friends like me. Being so far from you is hard, but I was so lonely here."

After a moment of silence, his father spoke up.

"Why can't you live in D.C. then? It's not as far. I'm sure there are gays there."

Michael laughed. "Yes, Dad, there are gay people in D.C. And yes, I could have moved there. But I had just broken up with a guy. I needed to start fresh—in a new city."

"Well, you can't very well move across the country every time you break up with somebody. That's just foolish," his mother added.

"You're right. I can't." Michael paused and said, "I'm sorry. I was expecting a very different reaction after telling you I was gay. I figured you'd be angry or upset. Don't you have any questions?"

"I can't say I understand it, son," his father replied. "But as long as you're happy, we're happy."

"I am happy, Dad."

"And you're healthy? You don't have that disease?" his mother asked.

"I'm healthy, Mom. I don't have HIV. I'm dating a guy, and we are being very safe."

That was the extent of the conversation. They had been supportive from the start, although they never asked many questions about his life in San Francisco, and Michael rarely offered any information. And here he

was, so many years later, asking if Scott could join them for Christmas. His family sensed this was a significant occasion, and they were thrilled. Michael had never introduced them to any of his boyfriends before.

On Christmas Eve, the lights on the tree twinkled, and carols played on the stereo. Michael glanced at his watch more times than he could count. Scott worked his shift at the hospital and promised to get on the road promptly afterward. Michael knew traffic would be heavy leaving D.C. and tried to be patient. When the doorbell finally rang, he sprung up from his chair to answer it. Standing at the door was the most handsome man dressed in a blue Oxford shirt and gray wool pants. His silk tie shimmered with stripes of blue and green. They stood motionless, gazing at each other, when a voice yelled.

"Come in already and shut the door. You're letting all the cold air in."

Startled out of their catatonic state, they entered the living room. Scott handed Michael's mother a bouquet and his father a bottle of wine.

"Thank you so much for letting me intrude on your Christmas celebration," he said.

Then he turned to give Michael a chaste hug. He moved his head to the side, but Michael would have none of that. He kissed Scott squarely on the lips, and his embrace gripped him like a vice.

"I'm so glad you're here," Michael said.

"We are, too, Scott. Now, let's go eat before dinner gets cold," Michael's mother commanded.

She set the table with festive Spode china and placed the flowers Scott brought in the center. Michael poured the wine while animated chatter filled the air. There was no formality to the gathering. People spoke all at once, hands reached for serving dishes across the table, and laughter filled their hearts as the food filled their bellies. Michael could see Scott felt right at home. His sister nudged him under the table, nodded towards Scott, and winked at Michael. She approved. He couldn't have been happier.

At 11:30, they piled into their cars and drove to St. Mary's Church for midnight mass. Although they didn't hold hands, Michael and Scott sat beside each other, their legs pressed together throughout

the service. At the sign of peace, they embraced each other tightly. With broad smiles, each member of the family wished them peace. Michael felt as if Scott had always been part of his clan. After communion, a soprano soloist sang his favorite song, "O Holy Night." When she approached her high note at the end, he grabbed Scott's hand and squeezed it. His eyes glistened in the low light of the little church. Michael couldn't hide his emotions as tears of joy streamed down his face.

•••

When they arrived home, it was nearly two in the morning. Michael poured a round of port for those still awake. Then, one by one, everyone went off to bed. Scott and Michael sat beside each other, enjoying the shimmering lights on the tree. The house was peacefully silent.

"Thank you for this," Scott said as he kissed the top of Michael's head. "This is the closest thing to a family I've had in years."

"You fit right in, you know. You're part of the gang now."

"That feels so good."

Michael sat up and pulled a box from under the tree. He held it in his hand and gave Scott a mischievous look.

"You're up to something, Michael," Scott said. "I know that look all too well."

"Perhaps."

Michael handed Scott the little box. He looked at Michael as he unraveled the bow and ripped off the paper. Resting in red velvet was a gold ring, set with black onyx and a diamond chip in the center.

"What the hell? Michael, you can't afford this."

"Shut up for a moment."

"Seriously, Michael."

"Shhhh."

Michael took his hand, placed the ring on his finger, and gazed into his eyes.

"Scott, would you spend the rest of your life with me?"

Scott was overcome with emotion. Tears flowed unceremoniously and wet their cheeks. How could he do this to Michael? How could he not?

"You crazy, impulsive, gorgeous man! What are you thinking?"

"Will you marry me, Scott?"

"Yes. I want to spend the rest of my life with you." He leaned down and kissed him. "As if I had a choice."

Michael's laugh nearly woke the rest of the family.

That night, their lives changed forever.

CHAPTER TWENTY-NINE
ROLAND
1993

Scott couldn't wait to tell Roland the news. He and Brian had witnessed the rise and fall of the Michael saga the first time around—watching him falling in love and soothing his broken heart when it came crashing down. They had always loved Michael, thinking he was the perfect match for Scott. While Scott thrived on schedules and order, Michael loved spontaneity. Michael wore his heart on his sleeve. One never had to guess what he was feeling. He posed challenging questions, sought deeper significance in people's behavior, and wanted to process their emotions. One had to pry feelings out of Scott—he was a master at keeping conflicting emotions in separate boxes. They were good for each other. Scott brought much-needed order to Michael's life, and Michael helped Scott get in touch with his inner world.

After breaking up so many years ago, Roland encouraged Scott to contact Michael. They challenged him when he chose his naval career over love.

"What use is a powerful career if you lose the love of your life?" Brian asked.

"He's right, you know," Roland jumped in. "You're lonely and

miserable without him. Your career won't fill that void in your heart, dear Scott."

"Maybe not," Scott said. "But I can't throw away everything I've worked for over the last eight years. Besides, I can't afford to repay my medical school loans without the Navy."

"Once you become a doctor, you'll do just fine with your bills," Brian said. "You and Michael are meant to be together. It'll happen. You'll see."

"Only if he stops being so pigheaded," Roland added.

Brian's words turned out to be prophetic. Scott's heart ached for him; he wished he were still alive to see them come true. At least Roland would understand. All their shared history made this turn of events even more profound. Their sadness and grief from his passing would make this celebration even sweeter.

Roland had contracted any number of opportunistic infections since Brian passed away. Scott worried he had given up hope that he believed there was nothing to live for. Even with his insane schedule, Scott made it a point to stop by, cook dinner, or just sit with Roland. Of all the things people with AIDS missed, the lack of human touch was the most difficult. Although the science proved AIDS could not be spread through casual contact, there was so much fear about touching someone with AIDS. So Scott made a special effort to massage Roland's shoulders and feet—he caressed his hair and rested his arm or hand on him as they watched TV. They had done the same for Brian, and now Scott hoped Michael would be by his side when his time came.

However, this wasn't the time to think about his last days. This was a time for joy. He hoped the news would give Roland something to look forward to. He always loved to plan parties and grand events. Perhaps he'd be willing to be their wedding planner.

Grocery bags in hand, Scott pushed open the door and clumsily made his way to the kitchen. After being away for the holidays, he was sure Roland could use a home-cooked meal rather than one from the meal service. Scott picked up fresh Maryland bluefin crab meat, old bay seasoning, and fresh veggies. Crab cakes were among Roland's favorite dishes. Busily preparing dinner, he didn't hear Roland enter the kitchen.

"The Prodigal Son returns," he intoned. "How was your visit with lover boy?"

"Hey buddy, it feels like I've been away forever. It's good to see you."

"Almost as good as seeing Michael?"

"Almost." Scott sensed an edge to Roland's tone. "You look good tonight. How are you feeling?"

"After a few days with the runs, I actually feel pretty good. Nothing like a severe case of diarrhea to help me lose those unwanted pounds."

"You had none to spare, my friend. That's why I'm here to fatten you up. How about some crab cakes?"

"Yummy! Is that bubbly, I see? What's the occasion?"

"You'll have to wait and see. For now, let me get dinner on the table. Sit down and keep me company while I cook."

Scott described his visit with Michael's family. He recounted every detail of the chaotic family dinners and Christmas traditions. He had never been to midnight mass before and asked Roland to explain the Catholic ritual. Roland was happy to oblige and shared memories from his childhood, including visits to the manger scene with Mary, Joseph, and the baby Jesus.

"You know that Brian and I met in the seminary? We were studying to be priests when we fell madly in love."

"Yes, I recall Brian was all too willing to share your sordid tales of clandestine sex. Scandalous!"

"You were always so uptight. Thank God you lived vicariously through our stories."

"Nothing wrong with following the rules."

"If I'm not mistaken, you were somewhat selective about which rules to follow, Captain Gay in the Navy!"

"Not for long. They moved my retirement up to April first. Then there'll be a party to end all parties."

"That's fabulous, Scott. We need to start planning right away!"

"Actually, that's a perfect segue for my big announcement," Scott said as he popped the champagne and filled the flutes. "My dear

Roland, would you do me the honor of being my best man and wedding planner?"

Roland's smile turned to a grimace. Scott was confused and worried. *Why isn't he cheering and toasting me? What am I missing?*

"Roland? Did you hear me? What's wrong? Aren't you happy for me?"

"Happy for you? Why would I be happy that you are leaving me for him?"

"I don't understand. I'm not leaving you."

"What do you think we've been playing at this last year? You come over every chance you get—you hug and kiss me. You massage my aching muscles and wipe my scrawny ass. You are doing everything I did for Brian. I just assumed you loved me."

"Roland, I do love you. You and Brian have been my best friends for years."

"You don't get it, do you? You're all I have. When Brian was dying, it was you and me taking care of him. And you've filled that gaping hole in my heart since he's been gone."

"But we never—Roland, I love you as I always have. How could I know you wanted more? I'm sorry, I… I don't know what to say."

"You've said quite enough. Since Michael came waltzing back into our lives in October, he is all you talk about. You've been so consumed with him you forgot about me."

"I never forgot about you, Roland. I have been here just as I always have. Can't you see how much I care about you?"

"Just not that way, right? I've heard this all before. You can't stand the sight of me. My body is wasting away, my mouth full of thrush, sores all over my skin. I disgust you."

Roland spit his words out like venom. His anger continued to mount, and his body trembled. His breathing became shallow, and he fell into a coughing fit. Scott leaped from his seat and put his arm around him, but Roland jerked out of his grasp.

"Leave… leave me alone. I can't look at you right now."

"Let me help you to your room. You're too weak to get there on your own."

"I might as well get used to it. You'll be leaving me soon enough." Scott reached out to Roland once more, but he recoiled. "Don't touch me!"

CHAPTER THIRTY
BROKEN
1993

He was catatonic as he cleared the table. Scott scraped the uneaten food into the waste bin and filled the sink with hot water. Washing the dishes had always brought him comfort. He loved the feel of warm, sudsy water on his hands. The immediate gratification of dirty pots and pans transformed into gleaming metal gave him a sense of control. It was a task. He took steps to complete it, and the results were immediately evident. There was nothing complicated about doing the dishes.

What had just transpired between him and Roland was far from simple. Scott tried to put the pieces of the puzzle together in his mind. How could Roland have assumed they were lovers? In all their years as friends, they had never had a romantic or sexual encounter with each other. They never even exchanged playful sexual banter. And yet, as he played the scenes of the past year in his mind, Roland's assumptions came into focus. Their time together was the image of domesticity. Cooking dinner, watching TV, cuddling on the couch—he could have perceived all of it as a marital relationship.

Scott was accustomed to taking care of people's physical needs. Although nurses did all the dirty work during the AIDS epidemic, much

of it was left to anyone willing to get their hands dirty. So many healthcare workers were unwilling to address their basic needs. Scott felt as if he were caring for his own family. These were his brothers lying untouched in hospital wards. His work became even more personal when tending to his friends. It never occurred to him that Roland had fallen in love with him. In many ways, their relationship hadn't changed at all. There had always been an emotional intimacy between them.

Of all the likely reactions he could have imagined, this cut him to his core. How could Roland believe he had betrayed him? He had to make this right, but he had no clue how.

In a rare moment of need, he dialed Michael's number. He had to talk to someone who would understand. Michael listened as Scott recounted every detail of the evening's events. He listened as Scott chastised himself for not seeing the signs, for being insensitive and cold. Then he spoke.

"Scott, you did everything right. You may have missed the signs, but you're not psychic. How could you know if Roland never shared how he felt about you?"

"True, but when I think about all the foot rubs and massages—I even laid with him until he fell asleep. All of it screams intimacy."

"It does. Don't take this the wrong way, but you've never been one to sense anyone's feelings. Roland knows that better than most."

"I suppose you're right. If it weren't for you telling me what's happening, I'd be clueless," Scott admitted. "It's just that I may have lost one of my best friends. What's worse is that I caused him so much pain when all I wanted to do was comfort him."

"You may have lost him, but that is his choice. Try to understand that you have no control over Roland's feelings. You can only change how you respond to him."

"What do I do now? Should I stop going over there? Should I leave him alone? I can't do that to him."

"Follow his lead. Let Roland tell you what he needs. But don't give up. Let him know you're still his friend, but don't push. Just be available."

"Thank you, Michael. I don't know what I'd do without you."

"Luckily, you won't have to find out. It's late there; try to get some sleep. Call me tomorrow."

"I love you."

"Love you too."

•••

Scott followed Michael's sage advice. It was essential to let Roland know he was still there for him. Over the following weeks, he followed his regular routine: buying groceries, cooking dinner, and cleaning up around the house. Roland's chilly reception did not deter him. Scott made a conscious effort not to force it. He didn't start any deep discussion about what had transpired at that fateful dinner. That part was relatively easy for Scott—profound emotional expressions didn't come easily. He reasoned Roland would talk to him when he was ready.

Thankfully, Roland's health improved significantly. He began to tolerate the drug regimen of AZT and gained a bit of weight. Not having to run to the bathroom with violent bouts of diarrhea meant that he could leave the house, take walks, and go on brief trips to the market. His improved physical condition positively affected his mood. Rather than ignoring Scott, he greeted him with bitchy comments. Scott read that as a good sign. After all, Roland had always been a bitchy queen.

On days he couldn't visit, Scott attempted to prepare meals that Roland could heat. He was in the kitchen chopping vegetables for minestrone, a hearty soup that would help soothe the sores in Roland's mouth and throat. He sang Michael Bolton's "To Love Somebody" as he moved around the room.

"Oh, honey, you know better than to do that."

"What? Do what?"

"My ears are bleeding, queen," Roland said, dramatically covering his ears. "Like I don't have enough suffering in my life!"

"Hey, my voice isn't that bad. You've wounded my fragile ego. I may go to my room and cry."

"Your wailing would certainly be an improvement over that singing."

The silence had been broken. Slowly, the icy wall between them thawed. At first, they simply exchanged playful barbs, but Scott soon

ventured into Roland's health. Playing doctor was safe territory. He could show concern yet be clinical, so there was very little risk. Scott was grateful for the detente and hoped they'd eventually warm to friendly intimacy again. A few weeks later, Roland made a significant overture.

"So, what horrid plans have you made for the big event?"

"Horrid? Once again, you underestimate my creative gifts," Scott said, clutching nonexistent pearls.

"Sweetheart, you have many gifts—creativity was never one of them. Now, tell Mamma all the sordid details."

"Honestly, the only thing we've planned is the date. We chose April 24, the day before the big march on Washington."

"Are you serious? Oh, honey, this city is going to be crawling with queens. Why in God's heaven would you choose that weekend?"

"Michael sings with the San Francisco Gay Men's Chorus, which is doing a joint concert with the D.C. chorus. So many of his San Francisco friends will be in town. Having the ceremony here in D.C. would allow them and our local friends to attend."

"All right, that's a good reason for the date and place. Tell me you've made plans. With all the events that weekend, it'll be nearly impossible to get a caterer, flowers, and music."

Scott grimaced and shook his head. Roland let out a disapproving sigh.

"You're useless! For God's sake, you're practically straight. And you wonder why we never allow you to take charge of any high gay events. If you're not careful, we queens are going to revoke your gay card."

"Does that mean you'll help us plan it?"

"Honey, I'm not letting you touch this event. I may concede to allowing Michael to have some input, but you? Absolutely not!"

Scott dropped what he was doing and engulfed Roland in his arms.

"Thank you, thank you, thank you! You have no idea how happy this makes me, Roland."

"Put me down, you big galoot! You're wrinkling my blouse."

"I've missed you so much, Roland. I never meant to hurt you."

"Hush now. Make my dinner. I have a wedding to plan."

CHAPTER THIRTY-ONE
WARNING
1993

  Lourdes and Kenneth were transplants to San Francisco—Kenneth was from Wisconsin and Lourdes from Florida. Kenneth had come to the city a year before Michael. They had been inseparable friends ever since. Back when Michael first arrived, Kenneth helped him navigate his transition. He introduced him to his friends and gave him a tour of the various bars and dance venues. Kenneth loved country music—Michael, not so much. But he convinced Michael to accompany him to the Wagon Wheel, a country-western bar south of Market Street.
  "You're going to love it. I promise," Kenneth said.
  "I'm totally doing this for you. I don't know how to two-step or line dance, but I'll watch."
  "Nonsense! We'll go early. They give dance lessons between seven and nine on Thursdays. After nine o'clock, the big guns arrive and take over the dance floor. That's when you get to see the genuine show."
  "Fine. I honestly don't know how you talk me into doing all this stuff. Soon, you'll have me dressed in leather chaps and going to the Stud."
  "Actually, that's next on your educational tour of San Francisco

gay bars. I mean, how do you know what you're into if you don't try it all?"

After his first evening at the Wagon Wheel, Michael let go of his prejudices regarding country music. Week after week, Kenneth and Michael met for Thursday lessons. Learning the two-step was easier than he expected. The line dances were so much fun that he yearned to learn more moves. But his favorite dance was the waltz. As a guy, Michael was used to leading. During the lessons, he learned to follow and lead with no particular preference. Still, Michael lacked confidence and would leave the dance floor after the dance class was over. By nine o'clock, Michael would find a stool at the bar and watch from the sidelines. The regular crowd of dancers overtook the floor, and Michael stared in fascination. They were so graceful. Then, one night, his spectator status changed.

"Hey, cutie, wanna dance?"

A blond, square-shouldered, handsome guy stood before Michael with his hand outstretched.

"Who, me?" Michael stammered. "I'm not that good."

"You underestimate yourself. I've been watching you for the last few weeks. You've gotten pretty good. So what do you say?"

"Sure, why not?"

Michael and his dance partner hit it off. The two-step turned to a line dance, then back to a two-step. When the music slowed with Laurie Morgan's "Something in Red," Michael's dance partner took the lead. He twirled him around the dance floor with gracefully fluid moves. Michael felt as if he were flying—he was in heaven. They danced for the rest of the night.

"You're a natural, Michael. My name is Stan, by the way."

"Thanks, that was so much fun."

"So, no more standing on the sidelines?"

"Thanks to you, not a chance. Will I see you next week, Stan?"

"Count on it."

Kenneth rushed over after last call, wanting to know every detail. Was he single? Did they exchange numbers? Would they see each other again? Michael felt like a girl whose dance card was full. He'd never been the popular guy at the bar, but that night, he was. And although country

music wasn't his favorite, he warmed to the sound of it.

•••

When Michael returned to San Francisco after Christmas, he could hardly wait to tell Kenneth and Lourdes his exciting news. He was engaged to Scott. They were happy for him but thought he was moving too fast. They also feared that he would leave San Francisco to move in with Scott. Kenneth was even more concerned about Scott's HIV status. He understood they would be fine if they practiced safe sex. However, his protective instincts kicked in, and he pulled Michael aside.

"I am so happy that you finally found someone you love. I honestly can't believe you're going to have a commitment ceremony."

"I know, right!? I never dreamed that Scott and I would ever get back together. It's not like I've been carrying a torch for him all these years."

"That's for sure," Kenneth said. "You've been a veritable slut since you arrived in San Francisco."

"I have not! Listen to you, pot calling the kettle black. You're the one who gave me the gay bar tour when I first moved here."

"All of that is true. Anyway, don't take this the wrong way. I just have your best interest in mind."

"Oh no. This sounds like it's going to be a big brother talk."

"Hear me out. I'm glad that you and Scott reconnected. I can't imagine what it's like to have the love of your life back in your world. But have you thought about what you're in for? I mean, really? If his T-cell count is as low as you say, you may have very little time before he gets sick."

Michael let out a heavy sigh and looked into the distance. These were the same concerns Scott had, and if he were being honest, he did, too.

"That's true, and a part of me is scared out of my wits. I don't know what's ahead. But I have no choice. I love him more than I love myself, and I can't imagine not being with him. Finding each other again—after all these years—it's a miracle. I am not sure how I will deal with him getting sick. I can't imagine having to watch him die. That I would be helpless as his body begins to break down, that I would have to

watch him suffer—it tears my heart in two."

"So why go there, Michael? He has a life back in D.C. with friends who can care for him when he gets sick. You have your life here, and it's really great. You've only been back in touch for three months. Perhaps you should slow down."

"I know it seems like we're moving too fast. I get that. The thing is, after that weekend together in October, something magical happened. It felt like no time had passed since we had been together. We only had to fill in what had happened in our lives since. We know each other—I mean—really know each other. What transpired during our years apart only brought us closer. I grew up and expanded my horizons. Becoming HIV-positive rocked Scott's world; it gave him an entirely different perspective on life. His priorities have changed."

"That all sounds great, Michael. But I am worried about you. I don't want to see you get hurt. And what about your health? Have you thought about what it will be like to practice safe sex even though you'll be married, sort of? You'll have to be hyper-vigilant about safety."

"I have to admit, I was anxious about it at first. But honestly, nothing has changed. Gay men have become accustomed to using condoms. It's just part of life. I promise neither of us will do anything to put our health in jeopardy."

"You better not because I can't live without my best friend."

CHAPTER THIRTY-TWO
RETIREMENT
1993

April was nearly upon him, and Scott looked forward to his retirement from the Navy with mixed emotions. He made his peace with his decision. It was the right time to leave. Given his health concerns and the life he and Michael planned together, he was content. However, having grown up in a military family, leaving his career behind was bittersweet. He knew that he would likely continue to rise in rank if he were straight. He'd have been able to marry a woman and continue to serve his country well into his sixties. And although President Clinton had recently been inaugurated, he was getting hammered by members of his own party on his proposal to eliminate the ban on gays in the military. Scott had little confidence the ban would be overturned. He didn't know how much time he had left and wanted to live the rest out in the open. Scott had enough of hiding in plain sight. Once he retired, they could not take away his much-needed benefits, and he'd be able to publicly proclaim his love to Michael. *I've finally gotten my priorities straight.*

Rather than have his retirement ceremony on base, Scott chose to have it at the hospital. When his commanding officer questioned him

about it, Scott explained.

"I have spent the last ten years trying to save countless lives in that hospital. Service to my country has taken the form of research and care for so many who suffered alone during their final days. My time on the AIDS ward took every ounce of energy from me. But when I held the hand of a dying man or comforted his partner, I realized that my life had meaning because of what we gave each other. The value of human touch cannot be underestimated. My heart was broken time and again on that ward. But it was on that ward that it was healed—over and over again. My retirement should be where my life's work came alive."

Scott's father and mother drove down from New York to celebrate with him. He was glad to have them there to support him. But the colonel could not understand why Scott chose to retire so soon.

"Son, you have a promising career ahead of you. Why throw it all away now?"

"I am a doctor, sir. Retiring from the Navy will allow me to pursue my research unencumbered. After the ceremony is over, we have a lot to discuss. Please trust me. This is the right time for me."

"You've always done the right thing, Scott. You will always have my support."

However, Scott wasn't so sure about his father's unwavering support. He had never come out to his parents, especially not while his father served in the army. He wasn't sure what the protocols were but didn't want to take a chance. Scott couldn't put him in a predicament where he'd have to report his own son. He was dreading the inevitable conversation. But this was his day. He'd been looking forward to this for months.

His co-workers gathered around, along with those of his patients who were mobile. His commanding officer began the ceremony and honored Scott for his years of service to the Navy and the many lives he touched. Then, one of the nurses sang his favorite song, "Simple Gifts," as she accompanied herself on guitar. Scott said a few words of thanks, then invited them to a buffet lunch. It was a remarkably uneventful end to his military career, but Scott was content. His only regret was that Michael was not beside him. *Soon enough, we'll be hand in hand for the*

rest of our lives.

• • •

Later that evening, Scott met up with his parents. He had made reservations at Crisfield's, a well-known seafood restaurant. His parents loved Maryland crab, and this was the place to get them. Scott's mother chatted endlessly about the retirement ceremony. She was disappointed that it was so short and hated that it was in a hospital ward. His parents would have liked a formal gathering at the base and were more than happy to share their opinions with their son. But Scott couldn't care less. His knee jiggled under the table. He was anxious about the impending conversation. Once the server removed the dinner plates and they waited for dessert, Scott broached the topic.

"Mom, Dad, I need to discuss a few important issues with you. You may find them difficult to hear."

"Oh, come on now, dear, don't spoil a perfectly delightful celebration with serious topics," his mother scolded. "Can't it wait for another time?"

"Actually, I've waited much too long already. The reason I retired so early is that I'm gay, and I want to spend my life with the man I love. His name is Michael, and we are having a commitment ceremony at the end of the month. I would like your blessing, and we would both like you to attend."

Both faces turned to stone. The long period of silence was broken by the server, who asked if they would like coffee.

"I'm sure this comes as a shock to you. I understand that is not what you had envisioned for my life. I've lived a double life for as long as I can remember. Life is too short to lie about who I am, especially now."

The colonel looked down into his coffee cup. Scott's mother laughed uncomfortably and fidgeted in her seat.

"You're kidding, right? You've always had girls chasing after you, Scott. I'm sure you'll find the right one. You spend too much time in the hospital with all those dying men. How can you expect to meet a nice girl when all you do is work?"

"Mom, it's not about finding the right girl. I've met the right guy, and I love him."

"Son, you know this is a sin. If you continue down this path, you'll go to hell."

Scott had always looked up to his father and sought to emulate him throughout his life. He couldn't bear the thought of disappointing him. Scott could see the conflict in his father's eyes—a mixture of sadness and revulsion. It cut him to the core. He understood their rigid worldview would not allow for a gay son. It wasn't in their lexicon and went against the conservative foundation upon which they had built their lives. The conversation was more painful than Scott expected. There was no use trying to reason with them. Scott decided he had better get to the tough news first.

"I have to share some bad news with you," Scott said, taking a deep breath before continuing. "I am HIV positive, and my T cells are dangerously low. I am not sure what my prognosis is. But you should know I may only have a few years to live."

"How can you say such a thing?" his mother asked. "You can't be serious. How could you have that—that disease?"

The colonel's face hardened. Scott saw he was struggling and hoped he would reach out to him. Instead, he wounded Scott more than he imagined was possible.

"This is God's retribution for living a depraved lifestyle," his father said. "What can you expect?"

Scott felt anger boiling inside him. His rational mind told him that his father was only parroting the conservative news media, but his rage won out. Never one to express extreme emotion, he couldn't let his father's insensitive remark go by. Still, he was afraid of making a scene. In a stage whisper, he placed both hands on the table and rose.

"How dare you judge me and my life? If you believe I deserve to die an agonizing death because of who I love, then I have nothing further to say to you."

Scott turned on his heel and flew out of the restaurant. The colonel and his wife sat in stunned silence as they watched him walk away.

Sitting in his car, Scott rested his forehead against the steering wheel. His body shook with rage and misery. *What the hell is wrong with them?* There was not one ounce of compassion in their response

to him. He expected them to have difficulty with him being gay, but his father's cruelty had gone beyond the pale. They can find their own ride to the hotel. How can anyone treat the people they love with such inhumanity? Scott didn't know if they would ever speak again.

CHAPTER THIRTY-THREE
THE FUTURE
1993

If there was one place in the world Michael loved more than any other, it was San Francisco. He was enchanted from the moment he first crossed the Bay Bridge on the last day of his cross-country drive. The oppressive heat of the Central Valley and Nevada was miraculously wiped away by the cool, foggy breeze of the city. Looking over to the Golden Gate Bridge, a bank of white clouds crept through the towers. Sunshine cut through billowing puffs and reflected off the skyline before him. The panorama was like nothing he had seen before—it was magical. Year after year, he grew to love it more and couldn't imagine living anywhere else. The mixture of bohemian expression, creative sophistication, and political progressiveness was a metaphor for his new life. Nothing was denied to him as he explored all the city offered.

Now, Michael was on the precipice of another life transition. Planning a commitment ceremony with his true love would have been a fantasy a few months earlier. They had both moved on, followed their own paths, and let go of a love that gripped their hearts. They had never stopped loving each other—quite the opposite. Their breakup was a heart-wrenching necessity in the face of Scott's military career. Despite

their love, neither was willing to compromise their dreams for the future.

Michael smiled as he reflected on the unexpected turns his life had taken. So now what? he wondered. Where will we live after the ceremony, D.C. or San Francisco? Although he loved his city by the bay, Michael would not let that impede their relationship. If they were to make a lifelong commitment, he'd have to learn to compromise. If Scott needed to stay in D.C. for his career at the hospital, so be it. Michael would give up his life in San Francisco. We could always move back when we retire, he reasoned.

Time was short, and Michael knew they had to discuss it soon. Up to this point, both had stealthily avoided any of the logistics of their union. The only planning revolved around the ceremony. Still at his desk, Michael dialed the phone, and Scott's voice reinforced every thought he had about compromise. He would live anywhere to be with Scott.

"Hi, my love. How was your day?" Scott asked.

"Just finishing up, but I wanted to catch you before you drifted off to sleep."

"My dreams wouldn't be as sweet if I didn't hear your voice to end my day."

"Aren't you a sweet talker? So, I was thinking about what happens after the wedding. I know we danced around this topic when you came out for Thanksgiving. But now we have a decision to make. Where would you rather live, D.C. or San Francisco?"

"Actually, I've been so wrapped up in planning my retirement from the Navy and our commitment ceremony that I haven't given it much thought."

"So, let me put this out there," Michael began. "I love San Francisco more than any place I've ever lived. But I also love D.C., and I will live wherever you want. I know your work at the hospital is incredibly significant. I won't ask you to give up another dream."

"Michael, you are my dream. Seriously, the only thing I want is to be with you—here or in San Francisco. To be honest, I'm ready for a change."

"You're not just saying that to appease me, are you? Because I am sincere about my offer to come back to D.C."

"I know that, and I appreciate how big a sacrifice that would

be. All I want is to spend the rest of my days with the man I love. We've wasted enough time because of my career. You are my priority now."

"How do you do that?" Michael asked, a single tear trickling down his cheek. "Here I am, crying at my desk. You know, I can picture us retiring in wine country and growing old together."

"I would like nothing better, my love. Maybe someday we'll have a home in Sonoma or Napa," he said, not believing he'd live that long. But he didn't want to ruin the moment.

"So, how do we make this happen? What's next?" Michael asked.

"I need to see if there are openings in San Francisco. If there is any place that could offer me the stimulation and challenge of AIDS research, it's there. But it may take some time. It might not be possible to move in together right away."

"Oh my God, Scott. That makes me so happy! I can ask around city hall. Someone's got to have a connection."

They chatted about neighborhoods they liked and whether they should try to get into the impossible real estate market or simply rent. The fantasy of living together became real in their imagining. Michael promised to mail Scott listings from Herth Realty on Castro Street. They hoped he'd be in San Francisco to celebrate Pride month in June.

"My only concern is Roland. He's been a real trooper helping to plan our ceremony. It's not like we're living together, but I've been stopping by several times a week to check on him. I don't want him to feel abandoned."

"He needs you, Scott. I get it. If you have to stay in D.C. longer than expected, so be it. You and I have survived living apart before."

"What did I do to deserve you? Thank you for understanding. We have a close group of friends here who can help. Perhaps I should chat with them."

"That's a great idea. They should begin visiting Roland now so the transition is more natural when you move."

"Good thinking. Leaving him will be excruciating. I just want to be sure he's not alone."

Their conversation meandered through details of their ceremony, guests in attendance, and living in San Francisco. Michael's heart was

filled with hope, and he dreamed of what it would be like to wake up every morning next to Scott. Although they had known each other for many years, they had never lived together. In a few short months, a new adventure would begin. He could hardly wait.

CHAPTER THIRTY-FOUR
WEDDING BELLS
1993

One could never guess that Roland had mixed feelings about losing Scott to Michael. If his feelings for Scott remained as intense as Scott suspected, he hid it well. Planning the impending nuptials gave him a new lease on life. He made lists for every likely need—florists, musicians, caterers. Every time Scott walked through the door, Roland would pepper him with questions, asking his opinion and trying to get his approval on decisions to be made. Scott appreciated that Roland was overcompensating for his unrequited love for him and was careful to give him as much attention as possible. But he was sure to keep the physical contact to a minimum. There were no more foot massages or cuddles on the couch. He didn't want to give any mixed messages. However, Scott was wiped out after a full day at the hospital. He only wanted to flop onto his bed and watch a mind-numbing sitcom. Roland would have none of that.

"Daffodils are in season in late April, but honey, I just can't stand all that yellow. It just won't work with the color scheme. I'd love to use pink and white peonies, but I don't know if they'd be available yet. Lilacs are lovely, and we can mix those with white narcissus. What's your

preference?"

"I love all of them."

"You must have a favorite flower. Help me choose something. What does Michael like?"

"That's a great idea, Roland. He'll certainly have a strong opinion. You should call Michael."

"Fine, I'll just have to plan this with him. You're impossible."

"I couldn't agree more. You know I'm not good at this stuff. Tell me the date and time, and I'll show up dressed and ready to go."

"Well, it's a good thing you're cute because you're useless. Do me a favor and dial Michael's number. I have to speak with him right away."

Scott smiled, listening to one side of the telephone conversation. There was a conspiratorial air to their interaction. He was sure they were both enjoying the Scott-bashing, and it made him feel good that the two most important people in his life were getting along. Michael had definitive opinions about the music. Since the gay men's chorus was giving a concert with the D.C. chorus, he arranged for several of his buddies to sing at the ceremony.

Together, Michael and Roland made all the arrangements for the big event. Michael labored over the language of the invitation. It wasn't a wedding, even though it was. Neither of them had heard of anyone calling it that.

"I thought we could call it a commitment ceremony. What do you think of that?" Michael asked.

"That's actually great. We are committing our lives to one another."

"Listen to this: Scott and Michael invite you to share in the union of their hearts as they commit to love each other for the rest of their lives."

"Will we have to pay union dues now?"

"Terrible joke. Seriously, what do you think?"

"I like it. It's simple, and it conveys that while we cannot legally get married, we are making a lifelong commitment. It's political without being political."

"You're right, though," Michael said. "The fact that we publicly

proclaim our commitment to each other is a political statement. Love is a powerful thing to fight. So, I have one more question for you."

"Sounds important. Shoot."

"Remember the priest who said midnight mass? You said he was a talented speaker."

"Yeah, he was a young guy, around our age. Father Patrick, wasn't it? What about him?"

"What do you think about having him perform our ceremony? Nothing is legally binding, but I think he'd give it the sense of solemnity I'd like."

"That's fine with me," Scott remarked. "But he's a priest. Is he allowed to officiate a gay ceremony?"

"As luck would have it, he's on leave. He may leave the priesthood because of the Church's stance on homosexuality and the lack of guidance in the face of the AIDS crisis. I'm pretty sure he'd do it if we asked."

"Go for it. I liked the guy. But does that mean we'll be married in the Church?"

"Well, even though he's on a leave of absence, he's still a priest. I wonder."

They laughed at the idea but were glad to have someone they respected lead their ceremony.

•••

On Friday night, friends trickled in—every time the bell rang, shouts of a joyful reunion resounded throughout the house. An excited buzz permeated the gathering—bursts of laughter, squeals of delight, and echoes of shared history as friends reminisced. Amidst the ebullient merrymakers, deliveries of flowers, wine, and extra chairs pushed through to the backyard. Anyone able helped set up lights or move furniture. Scott and Michael divided their time between entertaining and essential preparations. Pulled in all directions, the excited lovers locked eyes throughout the evening. A wink or smile told them all they needed to know.

Noticeably absent was Roland. He had done most of the planning—his list was posted on the refrigerator. He instructed both Scott and Michael to put a check beside each accomplished task. When

he got a moment, Scott snuck upstairs and knocked on Roland's door. He quietly opened it to see Roland lying in a fetal position.

"Hey, what's going on? Are you not feeling well?"

"What are you doing up here?" Roland chided weakly. "You have guests to attend to."

"Michael's got it covered." He placed the back of his hand on Roland's forehead. "You're burning up. How long have you had a fever?"

"Oh, I don't know. I woke up fine this morning, but by late afternoon, I lost steam—like all my energy had been drained."

"I don't like this. Let me get my stethoscope. I need to check your lungs."

"No, Scott. I'm breathing just fine. I've been overdoing it, plain and simple. I need a good night's sleep. Don't worry. I'll be good as gold tomorrow. Please, don't fuss over me—not tonight."

Scott shook his head and opened his mouth to protest when Roland put a finger to his lips.

"I mean it, Scott. If you ruin your big event because you're worried about me, I'll never forgive myself. Go! Go enjoy the party. Don't make me ask again."

"Damn, you're a pushy queen."

"And this is news to you? Get out of my room. Go!"

Scott did as he was told but sent people to check on him throughout the evening. Over-exhaustion and dehydration could bring on a fever. Scott wanted to believe Roland was right, but his gut told him otherwise.

Sitting in a circle of friends, Scott told the story of how he won Michael over for the second time. He recounted his speech at Dulles airport about not letting second chances go by, and a rallying "awwwww" rose from the room. Then Michael grabbed his face and kissed him.

"How could I resist?" he asked the gathering of friends. "I cried the entire flight back to San Francisco—five and a half hours! The flight attendant kept asking me if I was all right."

"You deserved it, my love, how you abandoned me all those years ago."

"I only left Captain Scott, not husband Scott."

"Very clever, but let's face it, you couldn't resist a man in uniform."

"Correction: I prefer you out of uniform!"

The party lasted late into the night. They ordered pizza and drank more than they should have. Aromas from the kitchen promised a feast for the following day. Roland hired friends who cooked for Glorious Food, a local caterer. They agreed to create a menu and do everything in-house to cut costs. The florist was also a friend—she employed every free hand to transform the yard into a romantic botanical garden. All of them joined in the festivities.

By morning, they were nursing their hangovers with large mugs of coffee. Michael and Scott played footsies under the kitchen table while they mused over the previous night's antics. The day had finally arrived, and they were more than ready. It would be hours before the ceremony, and they planned a leisurely day together: massages, haircuts, and a light lunch. Roland rounded the corner, greeting them with a bright smile.

"How are my two love bunnies doing on their wedding day?"

"Not too bad, considering how much we had to drink last night," Michael replied.

"You look much better today," Scott said. "How are you feeling?"

"Nothing a bit of rouge can't cover. I am feeling much better, dear. Now, let's look at our list, shall we? Oh, Lordy! The flatware and utensils! I had planned on ordering them but totally forgot. I don't know if they're open on Saturdays."

Scott jumped into action. Although he said he was fine, Scott wanted him to rest until the ceremony. He didn't want Roland to backslide into another episode.

"Leave it to us, Roland. We've got nothing planned today. You should stay close to home just in case some other calamity should befall us."

"That's ridiculous! I won't have you running all over town to find dishes on your wedding day."

"Scott's right, Roland. It'll keep our minds off things. Perhaps it'll distract us from our pre-wedding jitters."

Roland reluctantly agreed, and Scott was relieved.

"Thank God he gave in. I'm really worried about him."

"I know. Roland looks like he needs about twelve more hours of sleep."

"I'm sorry this throws a wrench into our day. I really wanted you to have a special romantic day."

"Being with you will make it so. Come on, let's scour the city. Maybe we can still make it for our massages."

Luck was not on their side. The party rental company Roland suggested was out of everything. There were events scheduled all weekend to celebrate the March on Washington. By noon, they had visited three others with no success.

"We may have to settle on paper plates and plastic utensils. It's not very elegant, and Roland will have a fit, but it may be our only option."

"No, we can't do that," Scott exclaimed. "Listen, it's a long shot but worth trying."

They pulled into the hospital parking lot, and Michael looked at Scott with confusion. Hopping out of the car, he trailed after Scott. Down to the kitchen, they went.

"You can't be serious."

"Why not? They have everything we need, and I'm pretty tight with the manager." Scott grinned.

Fifteen minutes later, they loaded crates of dishes, glasses, and utensils into Scott's car. After dropping them off at the house, they gobbled down a salad for lunch and raced to get their haircuts. They were giddy when they returned home, laughing at their wedding day adventures. They raced up the stairs to dress, with Roland yelling after them.

"You're going to be late for your own wedding. Get your queeny butts in gear and make yourselves pretty."

Gentle notes floated up into their room. The harpist played "There's a Place For Us" from Westside Story. The significance of what they were about to do struck Scott with full force. He glanced at Michael, fumbling with his bowtie, and felt his eyes well up. *How did I get so lucky?* Scott sidled up behind him and kissed his neck.

"I love you."

Michael leaned his head back against Scott.

"I love you too."

They took in the moment without rushing and looked at their reflection in the mirror. An energetic knock startled them as Roland flew into the room.

"Seriously, girls. Get it together. There's no time for lovey-dovey stuff. It's your wedding, for God's sake!"

"Isn't that an oxymoron?" Michael asked.

"Whatever, the guests are in the yard; it's ten minutes past three. You are fashionably late. Now get a move on."

Roland adjusted their ties, brushed a lock of hair out of Scott's face, and pushed them out the door. It was time.

CHAPTER THIRTY-FIVE
THE CEREMONY
1993

The harpist intoned "Che bel sogno di Doretto" from the opera La Rondine, and the soprano's heavenly voice soared over the garden. Together, they walked out to the deck and looked out over their friends and chosen family. Stands of lilacs dotted the yard's circumference, framing the guests. The cherry trees were in full bloom and hung like a canopy over a sacred space. Arrangements of pink and white peonies encircled them as they stood on the deck facing the guests below.

For the first time, Michael felt nervous. He knew Scott felt the same as they clasped each other's sweaty hands. The soprano soared into the heavens; her voice touched his heart and mind. I will promise my life to Scott in front of all these people. The thought thrilled him and left his heart exposed. To proclaim something so personal in public gave weight to the commitment. Michael felt his heart beating rapidly and realized that he was trembling. Just then, Scott squeezed his hand. Looking into his eyes was all he needed to calm him. Michael locked his gaze on Scott for the rest of the ceremony—he was his oasis amidst his anxiety.

When the music ended, the former Father Patrick addressed the guests gathered before them.

"It's not easy for two people to love one another. It's not easy when they are of the same gender. It's not easy to proclaim one's affection, attachment, and bond openly—for many are unwilling to see beyond their fears and celebrate the love we are here to witness today. We hope and pray that men who love men and women who love women will no longer need to fight for the fundamental right to love whomever they choose. And that someday, the myriad forms of love can be recognized and honored for what they are—embodiments of the divine.

"Each of us here has a responsibility to hold them up when life is difficult, to be here to celebrate each moment of happiness and joy in their lives, and to commit to walking by their sides throughout the journey they now begin."

Patrick then turned to Scott and Michael and addressed them directly.

"But what is commitment? The root of the word comes from the Latin mittere, to send. You send your word to another. To give my word is to 'place' a part of myself, or something that belongs to me, into another person's keeping. It is to give the other person a claim over me. It is now held by the one to whom I have yielded it. It claims my faithfulness, my constancy… not just because I have spoken it, but because it now calls to me from my beloved. What an incredible image. In making this commitment, each of you entrusts your promise, entrusts your life into the other's care."

Michael was overwhelmed as tears welled in his eyes and trickled down his face. Scott clasped his hands and gave him a reassuring look. It was time to speak their vows to one another. Scott graciously spoke his vows first so Michael could gain his composure. True to form, Scott's vows were cerebral and philosophical.

"Michael, I come here today to embark on a journey of wholeness and abundant life. We are created in an image of unconditional, unyielding, eternal love. We have within us the potential to share in this love if we embrace it as our life's work.

"It is my lifelong commitment to unfold this truth within myself so that I may share it unconditionally with you.

"I vow to foster this quest in you and to love you today and who

you will become tomorrow.

"To keep my eyes fixed on the truth that you are,

"Of beauty and of love,

"I promise to be ready at any moment to sacrifice what I am for what we can become.

"I love you in joy and in sorrow,

"And with all that I find within myself.

"Today, I take your hand in joy, with willfulness

"And I invite the journey we begin together.

"I consecrate myself to wholeness, truth, and life.

"I vow unyielding fidelity and,

"A lifelong bond of love."

One could hear a pin drop. The guests were mesmerized by the depth of his words. Michael smiled broadly through his tears. This was the man he would spend his life with. He took the binder from Scott and spoke his vows.

"Scott, I remember our time together as young men, playfully dancing with life's possibilities, not fully understanding nor grasping the fragile vessels we held in our hands.

"Time passed without warning, and our lives took different paths. We followed our dreams as they changed form. The successes and disappointments of life taught us more about who we are.

"And somewhere along the way, we began to love ourselves—enough to understand that we are worthy of being loved.

"And now we meet again, opening our hearts to one another.

"Now, with eyes that have seen life and death, we gaze upon two journeys that have joined once again.

"With eyes more perceptive and souls more aware, I welcome the fire of our newfound passion.

"Scott, I embrace the fullness of our love with all its pain and all its splendor. To you, I pledge my very being, confident in the creation of our two lives, joined as one."

•••

Patrick blessed the rings and led them through the rest of the ceremony. Then he asked those gathered to raise their hands toward

Scott and Michael and read the Apache Wedding Prayer written in their programs.

Now you will feel no rain, for each of you will be shelter for the other. Now you will feel no cold, for each of you will be warmth to the other. Now, there will be no loneliness, for each of you will be a companion to the other. Now, you are two persons, but there is only one life before you. May beauty surround you both in the journey ahead and through all the years. May happiness be your companion and your days together be good and long upon the Earth."

Not knowing what to do next, the happy couple embraced. Should we kiss? Will our straight friends think it's gross? What the hell, Michael thought. When they pulled apart, Michael leaned in and gently kissed Scott, and the crowd burst into applause. It was all so new to everyone. No one in attendance, including the grooms, had ever attended a commitment ceremony. They didn't even think to call it a gay wedding.

The day was filled with good food and jubilant friends. The remaining guests sat in a circle recounting the day late into the evening. Michael's brother launched into stories of their childhood that brought color to Michael's cheeks. That he and his parents were there at all filled him with love. Whether or not they understood, Michael's family was there to support them. He knew their religious beliefs taught that homosexual acts were sinful. Yet love came first.

•••

Alone for the first time since the ceremony, Scott and Michael retired to their room. They were physically and emotionally spent but couldn't wipe the smiles from their faces. Scott draped their tuxedo jackets on the back of a chair and turned to see Michael aimlessly fiddling with his bowtie. He came up behind him, wrapped his arms around his waist, and kissed the back of his head.

"Do I get to call you my husband now?" he murmured.

"Only if we consummate the marriage. Otherwise, it doesn't count," Michael joked.

"Honestly, I'd rather wait until morning. I can barely keep my eyes open."

"Oh, thank God! I can't wait to crawl under the covers and drift into la-la land."

"We have another big day tomorrow, too," Scott reminded him. "The march on Washington should be huge. They're expecting a million people."

"At least we won't be the center of attention. We can simply celebrate with everyone else."

Before long, they were spooning, and slumber stole them away. The following day was blissfully uneventful. Scott served coffee and muffins while Michael read through cards the guests brought. There were lovely gifts given and beautiful sentiments written. Michael read the card from his parents and looked up at Scott.

"How do you feel that no one in your family came yesterday?"

"I can't say I'm surprised. But seeing how supportive your parents were was like a dagger piercing my heart. I just emphasized the contrast. I know they love me, but I don't think they'll ever come to terms with my being gay. What hurts most is that they now know I'm HIV positive, and they've not shown one bit of compassion or concern. I cannot understand how anyone can treat their own child like that."

"I'm sorry, Scott. I don't know what to say."

"What is there to say? At least I have you. You're my family now," he said, reaching across the table to hold his hand. "You're all I need."

Then Scott changed the subject. He didn't want to cast a shadow on their day. He cleared the table and made plans to meet up with a crew of friends at noon. While Michael showered, Scott checked in on Roland. He had slipped away from the party pretty early, barely making it to dinner.

"Hey buddy, how're you feeling today?"

"Like I could run a marathon," Roland quipped. "Now leave me alone while I put on my make-up."

"Seriously, you don't look well. Can I listen to your chest?" Scott asked, stethoscope in hand.

"I suppose you won't leave me be until you do."

Scott placed it on Roland's chest and then on his back.

"You've got fluid in your lungs, and your breathing is labored.

Did you sleep at all last night?"

"I drifted in and out. I'm sorry to say I won't be joining you at the march today."

"Obviously. Listen, promise me you'll call 911 if it gets any worse. Do you mind if I call Dr. Jeff to check in on you today?"

"If it'll make you feel better. I'll be fine. I just need to rest. Please go and have fun. I can't bear the thought of ruining your celebration on the first day of your honeymoon."

"Please," Scott said, rolling his eyes. "It wasn't even a legal wedding. We gays don't get honeymoons."

"Be that as it may, you and Michael are married in the eyes of everyone who loves you, especially me."

"You're a love, Roland. Really. Please answer the phone today. We'll be calling to see how you are."

Michael and Scott were on the parade route with their buddies by noon. Michael's brother showed up with a t-shirt that said, Straight, But Not Narrow! Scott pulled him into a bear hug and thanked him for being so supportive. In return, he said, "Now you're my brother, too."

The crowd was dense, and the mood was joyful. Strangers greeted each other with smiles and kisses. It was a star-studded event. Prominent name performers graced the stage: the Indigo Girls, Melissa Etheridge, and Ru Paul made a big splash. As they were strolling around, Phil Donahue and Marlo Thomas passed by. Supportive politicians, including Nancy Pelosi and Jesse Jackson, spoke. However, what struck Scott the most was the contingent in the march that demanded the end of the ban on gays in the military. He teared up, knowing that his career was ripped from his heart. With vociferous backlash from Republicans in Congress, President Clinton had backed off on his campaign promise. Scott knew he had made the right decision to retire. He pulled Michael close and kissed him as the parade marched by.

That evening, they attended the joint concert of the San Francisco and Washington D.C. Men's Choruses. Michael didn't sing this time—he sat back and reveled in hearing his friends celebrate the great fight for civil rights through song. Part of the platform of the march organizers was to demand the passage of a lesbian, gay, bisexual, and transgender

civil rights bill. They fought to end discrimination by state and federal governments, including the military, and a repeal of sodomy laws and other laws that criminalize private sexual expression between consenting adults. One of the most essential demands for Scott and Michael was for a massive increase in funding for AIDS education, research, and patient care; universal access to health care, including alternative therapies; and an end to sexism in medical research and health care. On the weekend of their wedding, the gay community made history with the largest protest in American history. It was an auspicious beginning to their new journey together.

CHAPTER THIRTY-SIX
SAYING GOODBYE
1993

The fluid in Roland's lungs developed into pneumonia. He was admitted to the hospital the following Monday. There was little time for Scott to revel in the glow of his wedding festivities. Michael flew back to San Francisco first thing that morning, and when Scott returned from the airport, he heard Roland coughing. He immediately called an ambulance and got him checked in. Roland's energy level was so low he didn't even have a bitchy comment.

The following days were critical for Roland. Before HIV/AIDS, Pneumocystis pneumonia or PCP was rare. By the 1980s and 1990s, it was the most common diagnosis for people with AIDS. His doctor performed a bronchoscopy, where he inserted a tube into his nose and down into his lungs. The fluid was then sent to labs for analysis. Roland had presented with numerous opportunistic infections over the last year, but this was the worst.

Scott understood his prognosis was poor. He stopped in his room to check on his condition and sit with him. Even though Roland was weak and couldn't respond, Scott chatted with him about various goings-on. He read from the daily gossip column and shared his plans

for buying a home in San Francisco with Michael. His breathing became increasingly labored, and they put Roland on a ventilator by the end of the week. Scott feared this was the start of a rapid decline. The likelihood of coming off the ventilator in Roland's weakened state was low. Scott knew he had to prepare him for the end.

"Roland, sweetheart, I'm sure you know this, but things are not looking good. Your lungs continue to weaken, and your immune system is shot. It's time to make peace with yourself. I hate to have this conversation with you, but I want you to be prepared. I know you can't talk, but blink your eyes twice if you understand what I'm saying."

Roland blinked.

"I need you to know how much you mean to me. Knowing how much I hurt you when I told you about Michael broke my heart. I still feel a great deal of guilt over that. I hope you can forgive me."

Roland blinked.

"Thank you. I should comfort you, but here you are, helping me feel better. You have been an incredible friend throughout these years. You and Brian were—are—my family. I don't know how to go on without you in my life. Please know that I will not leave your side, and if a great miracle happens and you get well, I want you to come live with Michael and me in San Francisco. Wouldn't that be a hoot? You always wanted to vacation there."

He blinked again. But they knew that would never happen. Days dragged on, and Roland passed in and out of consciousness. Less than two weeks later, as Scott sat beside him, holding his hand, Roland became agitated. Scott stood and looked into his eyes. He looked angry, fighting to say something. His breathing became labored—they call it the death rattle. Scott stroked his hair and tried to soothe him.

"It's all right, my dear. I'm right here. I know you weren't finished here on earth. You have a right to be angry. This shouldn't be happening to you, Brian, or any of us. But your fight is done now. You can hand it over to me. I will fight for you and Brian. Let it go and be at peace. Feel how much I love you. Focus on that—how much we laughed and laughed. Think about Brian. Remember the first time you met—your first kiss? Picture that. Feel his arms around you right now. Remember

how much he loved you."

Roland's eyes softened, and his breath became less labored. Scott felt a slight squeeze of his hand before Roland closed his eyes for the last time.

•••

Scott lay his head on Roland's bony chest. He was gone, just like Brian, just like so many of their other friends and hundreds of patients Scott treated. So many young men, cut down like saplings, barely of age, with so much life to live, so much to give to the world. Over the years, Scott learned to numb the pain and distance himself so that he could be a good doctor. But that night, he wasn't a doctor. With his head on Roland's chest, he was just another survivor who had lost his best friend. A deep growl rose from within him—growing louder into a primal wail of grief. All those years of holding it at bay fed his bitter anguish. Scott sobbed with abandon, letting it all out for the first time.

Michael flew out the very next day. Scott knew he couldn't handle it alone. He handed the reins to Michael, who called the funeral home and church. He made all the arrangements and contacted friends and family. There was no wake. No one wanted to see what AIDS did to his body. At the funeral, a beautiful photo of Roland with mischief in his eyes sat atop his coffin. Michael got singers from the gay men's chorus to lead the music. The Irish Blessing had become a tradition—they had sung it at countless memorials. Scott leaned on Michael as they walked up the aisle of the church. He said almost nothing the entire day. Roland was the last of his close circle of friends to die of AIDS. Scott realized he was the only one left.

CHAPTER THIRTY-SEVEN
NEW HOME
1993

After Roland's funeral, Scott couldn't wait to leave D.C. He desperately craved a fresh start with Michael, and he needed something to look forward to. He gave notice to the hospital and sent his resume to contacts at the San Francisco hospitals. Even if he didn't have a job before moving, he was determined to start his new life with Michael.

He had hoped to find a position that would allow him to pursue his HIV/AIDS research while continuing clinical work with patients. Within a week, he had an offer from the medical school at the UCSF—University of California, San Francisco, doing precisely that.

Scott had moved into Michael's studio apartment in Diamond Heights by the end of May. It was an exceptionally foggy neighborhood, sitting just below Twin Peaks. The billowing fog tumbled over the hills and down into the city. From there, the views of the downtown skyline and the east bay were stunning. But when the fog rolled in, a thick blanket of white shrouded the apartments. Scott found the constant gray, cold fog depressing. He needed something to focus on—somewhere to channel his energy. The first order of business was to find a place to live. Scott had two weeks off before starting his position at UCSF, so he threw

himself into house hunting.

"I didn't realize how dark it gets when the fog comes in," Scott remarked.

"Yeah, it's especially heavy in this neighborhood. Just drive down the hill to Noe Valley or the Mission, and you'll find sunshine."

"You mean it doesn't cover the entire city?"

"Actually, no. Every neighborhood is different. Anything by the ocean is socked in, but there's usually sun on Bayside. Have you noticed they state "sunny neighborhood" in the real estate advertisements?"

"Yeah, I thought that was odd. So some parts of the city are sunnier than others. Can we please find a home in the sunshine? I don't think I can stand being in the fog."

"The problem is that they cost more. You know, we'd have a lot more flexibility if we rented. Are you sure we can afford to buy?"

"Look, I haven't had to pay for food and lodging while in the military. I have over ten years of savings. That should cover a down payment. Besides, at least I'd know that you are taken care of should anything happen to me."

"Don't go there, Scott. Please."

"I'm sorry, but we can't ignore it. Let's just see what we can afford. OK?"

Michael reluctantly agreed, which was all the motivation Scott needed. He scoured the papers and chose a real estate agent who gave him a tour of each district. They narrowed it down to the Castro, Noe Valley, and the Mission. They were sunny neighborhoods convenient for Scott's commute to UCSF and Michael's to city hall. Scott found the prices outrageous. He thought D.C. real estate was priced too high. San Francisco brought property values to a new level, and every property needed a lot of work. There was one condo that stood out, however. It was in the Castro district, the gay neighborhood. It was an odd property in that it had five bedrooms, and the list price was reasonable.

"What's the catch?" Scott asked the realtor.

"Five college guys are renting it now. It's a disaster. To be honest, most of my clients can't get past the front door. But the price is right. Shall we look?"

Scott was up for anything. He was desperate to get out of the foggy studio apartment. The realtor's warning had done the trick. He was prepared for the worst and set his expectations low. They entered from the garage and were greeted with piles of trash. Climbing the stairs to the unit, he noticed that the carpet was nearly black from the ground in the dirt. The condo was just as bad: it looked like a fraternity house with beer bottles strewn in every room and dirty dishes piled in the sink. The carpets and walls were so stained you couldn't tell their original colors. But the stench struck Scott the most—a mixture of dirty socks, beer, and cat urine.

"Well, you weren't wrong," he remarked to the realtor. "But it is spacious."

"Honestly, if you hire a decent cleaning service and give it a coat of paint, you won't recognize it. Wait until you see the view."

On the second level was an expansive deck with sweeping views of downtown and the Bay Bridge. It was unlike anything he had seen. When they got back to the real estate office, Scott called Michael.

"Can you meet me on your lunch break? You have to see this condo. It's disgustingly dirty, but it's nothing we can't handle."

They made an offer on it that day, and by midsummer, they were fixing up their first home together. They ripped out the filthy carpets, scrubbed the kitchen and bathrooms, and gave each room a clean coat of paint. Moving day was over within hours. Living in a studio for years, Michael had virtually no furniture, and Scott never had a place of his own. Michael's cozy couch and coffee tables were lost in the living area. The bedroom had a dresser, bed, and nightstands. But the rest of the rooms remained empty. They had virtually no furniture, but that didn't matter. They had a home of their own in the gayest neighborhood in the gayest city in America, and they were together. Scott's fresh new beginning was off to a beautiful start.

CHAPTER THIRTY-EIGHT
UNCERTAINTY
1994-1995

Michael and Scott quickly adjusted to the initial growing pains of living together. Both were dedicated to their careers and enjoyed success in their respective fields. There was never any downtime at city hall. Supervisors volleyed for media attention. Election cycles seemed imminent as soon as one passed, and the mayor was constantly under fire. Michael was in the center of the action, absorbing as much information as possible. Using his counseling background, he was adept at listening and making people feel heard. Michael found that staffers frequently confided in him or asked for his advice. He was careful not to step on any toes and deferred to whoever was in charge. His most well-known question was, How can I help? He was considered a team player who was open and honest—qualities in short supply in the political world. His hours were long, and he often had evening events to attend.

UCSF was just as stimulating for Scott. His goal was to maintain a healthy balance between his research and the clinical visits with his patients. No longer hampered by the restrictions of a military career, Scott could focus on finding a cure for AIDS. Results from a study of AZT during the early 1990s were disappointing. AZT was the only

drug widely used, but there were significant side effects. If one could not tolerate the regimen, there was no other option. In August 1994, he traveled to Yokohama, Japan, for the International AIDS Conference, but no breakthrough therapies or research papers were delivered.

Scott refused to give up. He spent long hours in the lab and with his patients, and sleep was a luxury. As to be expected, his frail immune system rebelled. One evening, Michael was dozing in front of the TV when the phone rang.

"Hello. No, Scott isn't here," Michael said.

"Michael, this is Doctor Liskey, Scott's colleague."

"Oh, hi. I'm sorry, I'm half asleep. What can I do for you, doctor?"

"Scott collapsed this evening while doing his rounds. We've admitted him to the hospital."

"Oh, my God. Is he OK?"

"We're doing some tests now. He's dehydrated and weak. We'll know more soon."

"All right. I'll be right there."

The hospital was less than fifteen minutes from home, but it was the longest drive Michael could remember. His patience was tested even more when it took him ages to find a parking space. He flew to Scott's room and poked his head in the door. He was sleeping peacefully, so Michael paused, trying not to disturb him. He took a deep breath. *Here we go. I'm not sure I'm ready for this.* As if hearing his thoughts, Scott opened his eyes.

"Are you afraid to come in?"

"Stop it. I didn't want to make any noise for fear of waking you."

"Please. This hospital ward is like Grand Central Station. It's a wonder anyone can get any rest in here."

Michael leaned down to kiss him, then moved his head so they were cheek to cheek. Pressing into him, his fear of losing him welled up inside. *Don't you dare! He needs you to be the strong one now,* he said to himself. Then he pulled up a chair and sat.

"So what's going on? Have they figured out why you collapsed?"

"Tests aren't back yet, but I'm pretty sure I know what's

happening."

"Of course you do. Your self-diagnosis is usually spot on."

"Promise me you won't chastise me for not doing something sooner?"

"No promises, Scott. You know you're impossible when it comes to your own health. Come on, give it to me straight."

"How about I give it to you, gay?"

"You're a regular comedian. Stop stalling and tell me what's going on."

"It's likely a combination of things. I've been working too many hours and not getting enough sleep. I should drink more liquids, so I am definitely dehydrated."

"These are all things I know. Get to the bad news."

"Over the last few weeks, maybe longer, I've been experiencing muscle weakness and sometimes cramps. It gets worse as the day progresses, and I become more fatigued. I believe it's myositis."

"Is this from your HIV?"

"Yes. It's not uncommon with people who have compromised immune systems."

"And what's the prognosis, doctor?"

"There's no cure, but there are medications I can take and, of course, physical therapy to improve my strength. I think they'll want to monitor me for a few days to ensure nothing else is going on."

"Scott, when will you realize that you're not invincible? I've been on your case since you moved out here. You never stop. I can't get you to take a weekend off, let alone a vacation. I'm worried about you."

"I know you're right. It's just that it feels like I'm giving in to this goddamn disease—like it's directing what I can and can't do. Somehow, taking a nap makes me feel weaker."

Michael rose from his chair and sat on the edge of the bed. He stroked Scott's head and gazed into his eyes. His hair was still jet-black, with a hint of a curl near his collar. Strong shoulders invaded the narrow bed with muscular arms resting on the sheets. Scott was the image of health and more beautiful than the day they met. But in his eyes, Michael could see fear, and his heart ached for him. *What am I going to*

do with this man?

After Scott drifted off to sleep, he made his way home. He plopped himself on the couch and stared out the window. He hated to do it, but Michael had to phone Scott's parents. In the months following their argument, Scott and his parents had come to a cordial but chilly relationship. His parents called to check on his health now and again and developed an amicable relationship with Michael. The mending of fences did not eliminate the conflict but lessened the chasm between Scott and his parents. Regardless of the tension, they had a right to know he was in the hospital. He dialed the number and held his breath until the colonel answered.

"Hello, sir. This is Michael."

"Good evening, young man. What can I do for you?"

"Scott collapsed at work today. He will be fine, but he's in the hospital."

"Good Lord. What happened?"

"Because of his immune issues, he developed a muscular disease called myositis. It causes weakness in the muscles around his trunk, like his hips, neck, and shoulders. He will need crutches and physical therapy when he gets out."

"Sounds like the prognosis is good, then."

"Yes. Scott is strong, and of all the illnesses from HIV, this one is manageable."

"All right, son. Please keep me informed. We'll plan to visit when he gets out of the hospital."

"I will, sir. Good night."

He hung up the phone and let out a groan. He was already emotionally spent. The very thought of having Scott's father come to San Francisco pulverized his frayed nerves. He couldn't let himself think about the colonel's visit just yet, so he crawled into bed and cried.

Their first two years together in San Francisco were filled with hope and new beginnings. In many respects, they lived life as if Scott's HIV did not exist. For Michael, the only hint was when Scott wanted something expensive or impractical. Without consciously reflecting on it, Michael would give in without a second thought. He believed that

Scott should have anything he wanted. It wasn't a morbid approach. He figured that there was no value in saving up for anything. Immediate gratification was their mode of operation. Who knew how much time they had left? If they wanted something, they bought it. Strangely, that attitude made for a very exciting life. Their friends marveled at their latest electronics or antiques. They stayed at luxury hotels and traveled to Europe both summers. His friend Kenneth joked that they were living the life of the rich and famous.

As Michael cried himself to sleep that night, reality sunk in. They couldn't ignore the inevitable. Scott's HIV had reared its ugly head and only promised to get worse. Michael had understood the road ahead would be torture. He just didn't think it would come so soon.

•••

The following morning, Michael stopped at A Different Light bookstore to pick up some magazines for Scott. Popular Mechanics and other science-heavy publications were Scott's go-to pleasure reading. Then he stopped at a florist—although he wouldn't admit it, Scott loved receiving flowers. It was still early when he passed by the nurse's station; the doctors had just begun their rounds. Dr. Liskey spotted Michael and pulled him aside.

"Good morning, Michael. How're you holding up?"

"As well as expected. So, what's the deal with Scott? Did you get any results back?"

"Yes, and it's not good news. I heard a crackle in his lungs and ordered a bronchoscopy. It confirmed what I suspected. He's developed pneumonia. That, in addition to myositis, is pushing his body to its limits. He had a rough time of it last night."

"Shit. How did he miss this? I mean, couldn't he tell he was getting sick?"

"Of course, he could. But you know him better than me. He can't admit defeat, so he ignored all the signs."

"You'd think he'd know better—especially because he's a doctor. So, what's the prognosis?"

"He's strong. But you need to brace yourself for a rocky road ahead. To be honest, this can go either way."

Michael wasn't prepared to hear that. Liskey was a friend. He told it straight, without sugar-coating the bad news. Michael was grateful for his candor, but at this moment, he wished for a shoulder to lean on. His pace slowed as he approached Scott's door. Peering in, he gazed at Scott lying in bed with an intravenous drip in his arm and beeping from some other machine. How did this happen so quickly? His handsome husband lay in a hospital bed, looking as strong as he always had. His shoulders were just as broad, and he appeared as fit as ever. With a day's growth, his dark stubble, and ruffled hair, no one could guess this sexy man was ill. Michael was lost in his thoughts when a thundering crash from the food cart startled him. Scott opened his eyes to see Michael at the door.

"Why are you standing there? Come in, already."

"I was fantasizing about joining you under the covers, you sexy beast."

"You're so full of shit, Michael. There's nothing sexy about me right now."

"You couldn't be more wrong, my love," he said as he kissed Scott hello. "I brought you a bit of reading."

"And calla lilies? What did I do to deserve you?"

Scott's voice was weak, and his smile was forced. Michael put on a brave face and sat on the bed beside him. Scott's breathing was labored.

"Take it easy, Scott. Dr. Liskey told me you had a rough night. Close your eyes and get some rest."

"In this place? It's so damn noisy, and they wake us up throughout the night to check vitals. Now I know why my patients can't wait to get out."

"I'm sorry, honey."

"Did Liskey give you the good news?"

"Yeah, you really are impossible, you know. Why do you ignore your own body? You should know better."

"I deserve that. I'm sorry."

They sat in silence, and Scott drifted in and out of sleep. Michael stared out the window, his mind wandering to dark places. Then he felt Scott squeeze his hand, and he turned his face towards him.

"Michael, you have to prepare yourself. This is only the

beginning."

"What are you saying? Stop that, right now."

"This is no time for denial. You know what lies ahead, and it's not pretty."

"Scott, please don't do this. You've got to fight. I can't lose you. I can't."

Michael rested his head on Scott's chest and let his tears flow. He could hear Scott's weak lungs struggling for oxygen. Scott's hand gently caressed Michael's head, and he knew he had to pull himself together. Drying his tears, he sat up and kissed Scott's cheek.

"Look at this—making it all about me. I'm sorry, Scott."

"Don't be. We knew it would come to this, eventually. I just hoped it wouldn't be so soon."

"Scott, you're talking like it's already over. You can't give up."

"I'm simply facing reality. I don't know how long I have, and I don't want to pretend everything will be OK."

"But it might. You've had patients recover from this before, right?"

"I have, but it's usually the beginning of more opportunistic infections. The body gets weaker each time, and T cells get lower."

"I know all that, but that doesn't mean you won't beat this. You are strong, and you can overcome this. Please don't stop fighting."

"I will never stop fighting, Michael. Because of you, I have so much to live for."

•••

Days turned into weeks, and Scott's condition continued to worsen. The cramps and pain in his muscles from the myositis kept him up through the nights. And while that gave him considerable discomfort, the more significant worry was his pneumonia. Rather than improve, his symptoms worsened. He developed a cough and a fever, and his breathing became shallow. Scott drifted in and out of restless sleep, but he'd ask about Michael's day or mundane questions regarding their condo when awake. Scott took Michael's hand one morning and asked him to sit on the bed.

"Michael, I feel like I'm losing this battle."

"Don't say that. You're going to get well."

"Please, let's not play games—not now. We may not have a lot of time. Can we just be honest with each other?"

"I'm sorry, Scott. You're right. I'm worried and scared."

"Please prepare yourself, baby. I know you don't want to hear that, but this is bad. I feel it getting heavier."

"I love you, Scott. Don't give up yet. Please promise me that."

"I won't. I love you, too."

Michael leaned in and gently caressed Scott's lips with his. Then he scooted beside him and let Scott rest his head against his chest. Michael lowered his head and kissed the top of Scott's head. Their idyllic life in San Francisco had changed in the blink of an eye. But for a moment that morning, nothing could come between them. By evening, Scott could barely breathe. Dr. Liskey recommended Scott be put on a ventilator.

"You realize he won't be able to talk with you. He's still lucid, so tell him what you need to."

"But… but… aren't his chances of coming off the ventilator pretty low?"

"It's over sixty percent. At least, that's my experience. Scott is stronger than most—there's reason to hope."

"I can't believe this is happening. I can't say goodbye yet."

"Michael, get a hold of yourself. This isn't goodbye. Scott needs you to be strong."

He took a deep breath and walked into the room. Scott understood what it meant to be on a ventilator—Michael knew that. He kissed him and told him he loved him. In a barely audible breath, Scott said, "Don't worry."

He's the one going through all this, and he's trying to comfort me, Michael thought.

The days that followed seemed endless. Scott was sedated so that he wouldn't choke on the breathing tube, but he seemed aware of Michael's presence. He sat at his side throughout the day and into the evening. Dr. Liskey came in each day to assess his progress. The good news was that his condition had stabilized. Yet he didn't believe Scott was strong enough to breathe independently. The longer he was on the

ventilator, the less likely he would survive. If he dwelled on it, Michael's thoughts grew dark. His only distraction was work. Lourdes or Kenneth came by with work projects and files several times each day. Occasionally, they sat with him or forced him to take a break for dinner or lunch.

"Come on now, Michael. You must eat."

"I'm not hungry, Lourdes. Coffee is fine."

"Do I have to get my girlfriend down here to force-feed you?"

"She loves me. She'd never do that."

"No? You realize she could hold both of us down at once. And you don't want to get on her bad side."

"I guess not. You know, you're lucky to have her, Lourdes."

"I am. And you're lucky to have Scott. Don't give up hope. You have to take care of yourself too, you know. He's going to need you more than ever when he gets out. What will he think if he sees Mr. Skeleton rattling around the house?"

He let out a little laugh and nodded his head.

"You're right. You're always right," he said as Michael let Lourdes lead him out of Scott's room.

Cafe Flor was near the hospital and was one of Michael's favorite haunts. Lourdes knew what she was doing by suggesting it. They ordered at the counter and found a little table outdoors. Once seated, both watched people walk by. Two young boys held hands and giggled as they passed. They were clearly in love or lust. Animated conversations filled the air while the Market Street traffic whizzed by.

"I'd forgotten how much fun it is to hang out here in the Castro."

"You've been holed up in that hospital room for weeks, Michael. You need to get out—just to clear your head," Lourdes said.

"Scott and I used to come here every week—it was part of our Sunday morning ritual. I don't know why we stopped."

"You guys are like old married folks. Keep the fire alive. Schedule a date night and bring back your Sunday ritual."

"You're right, Lourdes. If he survives this, we will do everything we always wanted to do. Why should we wait? Who knows how much time we have?"

"Scott is going to survive this, Michael. Please believe that. I've

seen you champion so many causes through your sheer positivity. Try to harness that energy again. You can't give up."

Michael felt the tears building behind his eyes. He had done his best to keep the depth of his emotions at bay. Burying his fears, Michael distracted himself with work and discussed the medical details of Scott's condition from a clinical distance. He was afraid that if he let himself cry, he wouldn't be able to stop. Lourdes reached across the table and placed her hand on his. That was all it took. Michael gasped for air as wave after wave of pain poured out of him. The other patrons took note with looks of sympathy. But it was not uncommon to see people overcome with grief. AIDS touched everyone in the Castro in some way. Michael's unmitigated emotional release consumed him. Lourdes rose from her seat, wrapped both arms around him from behind, and rested her cheek atop his head. She said nothing as she let him cry into her embrace.

"I'm so glad you're here, Lourdes," he said as his tears subsided. "Thank you."

"For what—for being your friend? You don't have to put on this image of strength. Stop trying to carry this load by yourself. Let me in."

When Michael settled down, he picked at his food until Lourdes gave him a dirty look.

"OK, OK, I'll eat."

Although he was embarrassed by his outburst, he was grateful to have let it out. The door was open, and he shared his fears and concerns with Lourdes. He needed a friend right now.

CHAPTER THIRTY-NINE
RECOVERY
1995-1996

Michael sat in his usual chair beside Scott's bed. Although he was mildly sedated to make the breathing tube less irritating, the nurses told him to talk to him. He wasn't sure how much Scott retained, but he was determined to stimulate his brain. He found a trashy gay romance novel at A Different Light bookstore and read to him for hours. He was reading a saucy scene when Dr. Liskey entered the room. Looking up, he noticed a smile on the doctor's face.

"Well, now, that should certainly get a rise out of him."

"Hey, he'll be out of practice when he gets out of here. I intend to keep his brainwaves stimulated."

"Among other things," Liskey said with a chuckle.

"How's he doing today?"

"Actually, Scott's numbers are good. We'll start weaning him off the oxygen today. I don't think he needs as much sedation either, so we'll reduce that as well. He should be more aware of what you're saying, so be nice."

"Oh, my God. That is great news. How long will it take to get him off the ventilator completely?"

"It all depends on how he responds. If he transitions smoothly, it can be a matter of days—perhaps less. This has been a rough couple of weeks, but Scott has been stable for several days. Looks like he's beat the odds. Let's hope his lungs get used to breathing on their own."

Michael's heart swelled. He had kept his emotions at bay—not letting himself descend into despair or be too hopeful. His relief and joy burst forth without warning. He jumped up and engulfed Dr. Liskey in a bear hug, and tears streamed down his cheeks.

"I know, Michael. I know. These last weeks have been torture. Just let it out."

Later that day, Michael noticed Scott's hand reaching out for him. He was awake. Michael sat on the bed and stroked Scott's hair. Scott squeezed his other hand.

"Hey, my love. Where've you been?"

Michael leaned in and kissed his forehead.

"You're doing well. They reduced your oxygen, and you've been breathing better. Maybe they can remove the tube tomorrow or the next day."

Scott blinked and squeezed Michael's hand again.

"Yeah, I know. I love you too," Michael said. "I've been so worried about you. I can't wait until you can speak again. I just want to take you home."

The next day, Scott's condition continued to improve, so Dr. Liskey removed the breathing tube. He coughed, and his throat was sore, but Scott was breathing on his own after three weeks on the ventilator. It was a miracle. At least, that's what Michael believed. In the days that followed, Scott gained strength, and they had him up and walking as much as he could tolerate.

Michael placed another call to his parents to let them know his status. He didn't expect the response he got when he told them he'd be coming home from the hospital.

"Can you take time off to care for him?" the colonel asked.

"No, sir. I've missed so much while he's been in the hospital. I can't take more time off. But I work close by. I can stop by and check on him throughout the day."

"Well, that won't work. I'll check the flights and let you know. I'll come to stay during his recovery."

Michael was panicked. That was the last thing he wanted.

"That's unnecessary, sir. I've got this, really."

"Nonsense. I'll call you as soon as I confirm my flight."

Michael hung up the phone and groaned. He hoped he could avoid the colonel's visit. He was already emotionally spent. Maybe it won't be so bad. At least Scott won't be alone all day, and I could use the help.

•••

It all happened at the same time. Michael picked up Scott from the hospital and got him settled into their bedroom. Unfortunately, it was up a flight of stairs. A couple of hours later, he was at the airport waiting for the colonel's flight. Michael hoped for a few nights at home alone before the colonel's visit, but that wasn't to be. He resigned himself to making the best out of their circumstances. In-laws were in-laws, gay or straight. There was nothing unique about having a strained relationship with them.

In general, Michael's rapport with the colonel was familiar but formal. He never made small talk, and after a while, Michael stopped trying to fill the silence with useless chatter. On the way home from the airport, the colonel peppered him with questions about Scott's health and recovery. He didn't expect many details; he simply wanted to know if his son would be all right. Michael could feel his pain and that, despite his judgment about being gay, he loved Scott. Michael understood it was all he was capable of, and he would meet him where he was—no expectations.

The following week was hectic for Michael. He had taken more time off than he had throughout his entire time at city hall. Fortunately, his co-workers understood and covered for him. His priority was Scott. All else would have to wait. Each night, he changed out of his work clothes, set the table, and prepared dinner. During the first few nights, Scott was in too much pain to tackle the stairs down to the kitchen. So Michael made the plates and served the colonel. Then he fixed a tray and brought dinner up to Scott. By the third night, while Michael was at the

stove, he heard a commotion.

"What are you doing coming down all these stairs by yourself, son? You should have called for help."

"I'm fine, Dad. I needed to get out of my room for a bit."

"Scott, are you all right?" Michael jumped in. "Here, let me give you a hand."

"Both of you, just stop! I feel like I'm living in a fishbowl," Scott yelled. "Leave me be. I can manage on my own."

Scott rarely raised his voice. Michael and the colonel were stunned into silence. Michael backed away and continued cooking dinner as Scott sat at the table. The colonel put the TV on, and they watched the local news while Michael finished up. By the time dinner was served, the tension had broken. Michael moved to the sink and began cleaning up the dishes. When he turned to wipe the table, he noticed Scott was sitting alone. The colonel had gone to his room.

"Hey, I'm sorry. I didn't mean to snap at you earlier."

"No need to apologize, Scott. You're in pain, and you're a terrible patient. You always have been."

"Nice. Knock a guy when he's down. You're right, though. I hate feeling helpless and having to rely on everyone. And with you guys being so nice and attentive—I don't know."

"I'm sure the medication you're on makes you a little foggy, too," Michael said. "But you have to let me help. It's either your father or me."

"Sure, threaten me. All right then, help me up the stairs to our room?"

"It'll be my selfish pleasure," Michael said as he extended his arm.

During his first days out of the hospital, Scott spent most of his time in bed. That left Michael to entertain the colonel. Each night, they'd sit at the dinner table in relative silence. He answered questions and gave instructions regarding Scott's care. One night, after several martinis, the colonel's guard was down.

"I'll never understand why you took him away from the navy. None of this would have happened."

"What did you say?" Michael asked in a measured voice.

"Scott had a brilliant career ahead of him," the colonel slurred. "Then he got mixed up in all this gay nonsense."

"Are you accusing me of making your son gay? You think he left the Navy because of me?"

"He was fine before you came around."

"You are an ignorant bigot, and you are in my home. How dare you speak to me that way?"

The colonel drew back in shock. Michael was always kind and gentle. The colonel didn't know how to react. But Michael had enough. He let his anger and frustration out.

"If you had more than two drunk brain cells in your head, you'd know that Scott has always been gay. Though I'd like to take credit for his sexuality, I don't have that power. You and your limited worldview let this virus spread unchecked for years. Thousands of people died before the government took any notice. Why? Because it was happening to throwaways—gay men and IV drug users. Who cares about them? Let them kill each other off. That will solve the problem. In your callowness, you've blinded yourself from seeing how happy your son is—how in love he is with me and I with him. You haven't noticed that we have a better marriage than either of your other sons. Being gay has nothing to do with it. But you can't see that, can you? You sit in judgment of us, shrouded in the shadow of ignorance, while Scott battles this disease every day. Rather than cherish the time you have with him, you push us both away. I should throw you out of our home right now. For Scott's sake, I will pretend everything is fine and dandy. But don't you ever dare to degrade me or my relationship with Scott, not while you're in my house."

The colonel cowered in speechless silence. He was rarely bested by anyone, let alone Michael. He rose from the table and staggered to the door. Barely audible, he said, "I'm sorry." Then he went off to bed. The cordial rapport they enjoyed turned to chilly avoidance, but nothing further was said.

Scott slowly gained strength in his muscles over the next week. He sat at the dinner table almost every night after that, although he needed help climbing the stairs. By the end of his two-week visit, the

colonel had clearly overstayed his welcome. He had come to help take care of Scott. Instead, Michael ended up taking care of both him and Scott. He prepared all their meals, washed the dishes, and did the laundry. When he came home from work, there was a dirty pile in the sink from breakfast and lunch. Michael's patience was wearing thin. He finally spoke up.

"Colonel, would you mind clearing the table after dinner tonight? I'm wiped out, and I just finished cleaning up after you two. I can't look at another dirty dish."

Scott raised a brow and flashed an amused look at Michael. The colonel took the hint. When he returned from work the next day, the sink was clean, and he helped set the table for dinner. Scott always said the colonel respected strength. He was pleased that Michael let him catch a glimpse that night. One did not take advantage of Michael's kindness—not if they wanted to live to tell the tale. However, Scott had no idea what had transpired a few nights before. When Michael dropped the colonel at the airport, he took his bags from the trunk and held out his hand. The colonel's firm grip pulled him in for a stiff hug.

"Thank you for taking care of my son," he said. "We love you."

Then he turned and walked into the terminal. Michael stared after him in disbelief. *Did that just happen? Maybe I got through to him after all,* he thought.

During the following weeks, Scott's strength improved dramatically. He could return to work, albeit on a modified schedule. From then on, Michael monitored his hours. A couple of months later, his health was back to normal. Michael knew they had dodged a bullet with Scott's myositis. However, he knew Scott could fall ill at any time, especially if he pushed himself too hard. As the months passed, he remained on edge.

• • •

After his bout with PCP and myositis, Scott was fortunate not to have any further issues. Michael made sure dinner was on the table each night. Skipping meals was not an option. Their daily routine was remarkably ordinary: dinners, watching television, and bedtime by 11:00 p.m. Scott appreciated Michael's diligence regarding his health

and gladly followed his lead.

Years of seemingly no progress plagued the gay community. Unlike viruses like the common cold, HIV is a retrovirus that tricks cells into making copies of itself. As it multiplies, there are fewer healthy cells, resulting in a lifelong infection. For years, the only drug to treat HIV was AZT, which was highly toxic and resulted in serious side effects. Scott's biggest fear was that he would develop resistance to the drug. If that happened, the virus, which mutated easily, would make a renewed attack on his healthy cells. He dreaded getting his blood work done. Each time, he held his breath until the results came back.

By the mid-nineties, only a couple of years after his myositis episode, there was a significant breakthrough. Scott was part of a research team that discovered a regimen of drugs to slow the replication of HIV. The researchers called these protease inhibitors the HIV cocktail. It was the first breakthrough in many years, and he couldn't wait to tell Michael the news.

That night, Scott made reservations at Bacco, their favorite neighborhood restaurant. He left a message for Michael to meet him there at seven. Scott sat at their usual corner table with a bottle of Cristal Champagne resting in an ice bucket. Michael walked in carrying all the day's stress and spotted Scott looking like the Cheshire Cat.

"What's with that silly grin? Champagne? What's going on?"

"Lots of questions, Michael. How about a kiss hello?"

Michael abided by Scott's request and sat.

"OK, spill it. I can't stand the suspense."

"It looks like it's going to get emergency approval. You know, the drug cocktail we've been studying. This is a game-changer, Michael."

"Oh, my God. That's amazing. What does that mean in practical terms?"

"You know how toxic AZT is, right? And that many people with AIDS develop a resistance to it? Well, this new combination of three drugs significantly reduces the cell's ability to produce HIV. In practical terms, it will extend the lives of people with HIV and AIDS. This is huge, Michael."

They toasted to science and to hope.

The initial results were promising, and the drugs were approved in 1996. The new cocktail completely changed Scott's quality of life. He no longer experienced night sweats and constant diarrhea. The regimen was demanding, requiring him to take it three times a day on an empty stomach, often resulting in abdominal issues. But he understood the science and knew the cocktail would keep him alive longer.

Regular visits to his physician became routine rather than something he dreaded. For the first time since his diagnosis, Scott looked to the future with a hint of optimism.

CHAPTER FORTY
NEW MILLENNIUM
2000

Everyone was obsessed with doomsday predictions for the new year. It was called the Y2K bug. The world's computer systems were programmed without the first two digits of the year. 1990 would be written as 90. The fear was that come January 1, 2000, programs would read 00 as 1900 rather than 2000. There were fears that data would be lost. Banks would not be able to calculate interest. Rumors spread that nuclear missiles in Russia and the US would mistakenly misfire and power plants would fail. Big cities across the globe planned grand celebrations to usher in the new millennium. Amid the rumors, there was great hope and desire to celebrate.

Michael and Scott looked forward to the event with great excitement. Friends had invited them to spend New Year's Eve on a sailboat. With only three couples, it would be an intimate gathering.

"I can't believe Duncan and Jeff invited us to spend New Year's Eve on their boat," Michael said.

"Why wouldn't they? They're our closest friends. Besides, we're part of the "A gay" crowd, aren't we?"

"Maybe the B or C crowd, but we're still lots of fun. So, I guess

we qualify. What shall I wear? It'll be chilly on the bay, especially at that hour."

"Michael, you'll look fabulous no matter what you wear."

"You're such a charmer. Some things never change."

Their excitement was palpable. Michael had purchased six champagne flutes, the year 2000, etched in the crystal. They were way over budget, but he had to mark the special occasion. He reasoned they would be a lovely gift to Duncan and Jeff for inviting them. Scott and Michael boarded the sailboat at a marina in Brisbane, just south of the city. It was a mild, clear evening with the perfect wind for a leisurely sail. Heading north toward the Bay Bridge, Michael squealed with delight as the twinkling lights of the city skyline came into view. Even after all these years, Scott got a kick out of Michael's childlike wonder. It never failed to draw him into the moment, feeling every bit of Michael's excitement.

Although they had been sailing with Duncan and Jeff before, their New Year's cruise offered spectacular views of San Francisco at night. Sailing under the Bay Bridge was thrilling. Reflecting on the bay, the Transamerica and Embarcadero buildings were festively lit for the holidays. Duncan loved Michael's energy and asked if he wanted a turn at the helm. Scott saw the glint in his eyes. He would never refuse.

"You want to feel the wind at just the right angle, Michael. If you monitor the gauge, it will show you what direction it's coming from. Just keep the needle in that gray range, and you'll be fine."

"Is it normal for the boat to heel so much?" he asked as it tilted to one side.

"Yes, it won't tip over. If the wind blows too hard, turn slightly to let some wind out of the sails."

That was all Michael needed to hear. His love of adventure kicked in, and he sailed like a pro. As they approached the Golden Gate Bridge, the wind grew stronger. Michael leaned into it with a toothy grin on his face.

"Easy there, my love," Scott warned. "Let's not get cavalier. Why don't you let some of the wind out of the sail? We're heeling a bit too much for my comfort."

"Aw, you're such a killjoy. I was just having a little fun."

For dinner, they anchored in a placid cove by Treasure Island. Duncan had prepared an elegant feast, starting with cocktails on the deck, followed by seafood chowder in sourdough bowls as an appetizer, and for the entrée, individual beef Wellingtons with asparagus wrapped in crispy bacon. The dessert was a rich chocolate mousse topped with whipped cream. Before long, it was time to go up on deck to ring in the new year. The champagne flutes were a big hit, and they filled them with Dom Perignon. At the stroke of midnight, the sky lit up with a magnificent display of fireworks. The evening could not have been more perfect.

•••

After the fireworks, while everyone chatted on deck, Scott wandered onto the bow of the boat. With his champagne in hand, he stole a moment alone. The waves lifted the boat up and down— its gentle rhythm coaxed tears from his eyes. Scott had made it to the new millennium. He could hardly believe it. He would turn forty in the year 2000. He never dreamed he'd make it to thirty-five. When he and Michael got married in 1993, he fully expected that he'd die within the following year. But here he was, not just alive but thriving. He was happier than he'd ever been. He felt a hand on his back, then Michael's chin rested on his shoulder. They gazed at the San Francisco skyline without exchanging words. It was a decisive milestone, and they both understood the impact.

"What's going through that head of yours?" Michael finally asked.

"Oh, nothing. Just thinking."

They listened to the lapping water on the bow of the boat. The sounds of the city echoed across the bay, and the cool breeze let them know they were in San Francisco.

"You know I love you," Scott said at last.

"And I love you," Michael replied.

Michael nestled under Scott's shoulder, and they stood together, wondering what the future would bring. *Maybe I should start thinking about living rather than preparing to die,* Scott thought. It was a paradigm shift. The past ten years had been focused on death. Now it was time to let that go, start a new chapter, and embrace life.

CHAPTER FORTY-ONE
WEDDING AT CITY HALL
2004-2015

    Michael was a fixture around city hall. Having worked for supervisors and several mayors, they knew him to be levelheaded and results-oriented. He never allowed himself to be blinded by any singular political ideology. In a progressive city such as San Francisco, he found he could agree on foundational levels with every candidate or politician. Whether they were left- or right-leaning was relative. They were all liberal. That approach made him a favorite confidant for many of the city's leaders. He had his finger on the pulse of the mayor's thoughts, and they always knew they would get a straight answer from Michael.
    From 1996 to 2004, Michael was deputy chief of staff for the infamous Willie Brown. He was a powerful figure in California politics and was speaker of the State Assembly before becoming the first Black mayor of San Francisco. Brown was a dashing figure whose political savvy was only rivaled by his charm. Michael loved working for him. He observed his every move and took note as he handled the many people who sought favors. One of his fondest memories was when Mayor Brown kept the Archbishop of San Francisco waiting simply to show who was in charge.

He and the board of supervisors created a policy requiring anyone doing business with the City of San Francisco to offer health care benefits to domestic partners. The Catholic Church did not recognize same-sex couples as domestic partners. However, it didn't want to jeopardize the thousands of dollars it received from the city. By the end of the meeting, the archbishop had agreed to offer benefits with a much broader scope. Brown had broadened the definition of domestic partner to include next of kin, such as a child caring for an elderly parent. As long as it wasn't strictly limited to gay and lesbian couples, the archbishop could save face and agree to the policy. Brown was a true powerbroker who understood how to get the results he desired. He took Michael under his wing and groomed him as the next chief of staff. His efforts paid off when the next mayor of San Francisco, Gavin Newsom, appointed Michael to that post.

In 1993, the same year Michael and Scott had their commitment ceremony, the fight for marriage equality gained ground. The Supreme Court of Hawaii ruled that same-sex marriages could not be denied unless there was a compelling reason. That ruling fueled a backlash throughout the country. Fearing other states would have to recognize legal same-sex marriages from Hawaii or any other state that might legalize it, Congress wrote a law called the Defense of Marriage Act, DOMA. Disappointing the gay community once again, President Clinton signed it into law. It allowed states to ignore legal marriages from other states based on sex and stated that the federal government did not have to recognize same-sex marriages. For all his talk about supporting equal rights for the gay community, he did more damage than good to a constituency that helped get him elected.

Michael watched the national fight for marriage equality with great personal interest. However, there was an element that he could not let go of. He had always believed in activism and fighting for recognition and rights. And while the validation of a legal marriage certificate would be a milestone, he understood that it was much more. Without that legal recognition, he could not care for Scott should he become incapacitated. That was one of his greatest fears. As a couple, they didn't have the legal protection that straight married folks had—one's spouse is considered the

closest relative. Since Michael was not Scott's legal husband, he was not next of kin. If Scott was incapacitated, his parents could come swooping in and take him away. They could make medical decisions for him. It wasn't a far-fetched fear. It had happened time and again to friends of theirs. Given the animosity and judgment Scott's parents showed when he came out to them, he expected the worst.

The other issue was health care. If Scott was unable to work, he might lose his health insurance. If they were legally married, Michael could add him to his policy. The practical repercussions were not insignificant. The argument that marriage was a religious matter distracted many people.

The issue was being batted around between state legislatures and the courts. Several states voted for bans against same-sex marriages, including Nevada, Alaska, and Hawaii. In 2003, Vermont and Massachusetts used the courts to legalize it based on anti-discrimination laws already in the constitution. The state of California passed a domestic partnership law that gave same-sex couples virtually the same state benefits as married couples. When Michael's new boss, Mayor Newsom, told him he wanted to perform marriages at city hall, he thought he was crazy.

"Mr. Mayor, that's political suicide," Michael told him, even though the very idea thrilled him. "This is your first year in office. Are you sure you want to die on this hill?"

"Michael, are you telling me you and Scott wouldn't want your union to be officially recognized as a marriage?"

"Of course, I would. Without legal recognition, we are not protected. But I know you have bigger plans beyond being mayor of San Francisco. The Mormons and the Catholic Church successfully killed the issue in Hawaii. They have honed their skills along with the religious right. It would be difficult to set your sights on the governor's mansion with those major lobbies fighting against you."

"Spoken like a loyal chief of staff. You know you are trying to convince me to go against your best interest, don't you?" the mayor said.

"I do, and it's like a punch in the gut. I would give anything for marriage equality to be the law of the land. But I honestly don't think it's

the right political move for you."

"But it is the right thing to do from a moral perspective," Newsom stated.

Michael was floored. He found himself arguing against something he truly believed in. And here was the mayor speaking with such conviction. Newsom was a privileged, white, straight male, yet he was willing to endanger his political career over gay marriage. When he relayed the conversation to Scott that evening, he questioned Michael's perception.

"I know you have a great deal of respect and admiration for him, Michael. But don't you think he is taking a calculated risk? He'll be hailed as a hero in San Francisco and progressive circles all over the state."

"He would. But the religious right and conservatives believe the domestic partnership law already covers the equality issue. Most people believe the term marriage should be reserved for a man and a woman. They use quotes from the Bible. They've equated marriage with a sacramental or religious commitment."

"Be that as it may, Newsom is not an ignorant man. He must suspect there'll be some political benefit."

"Honestly, I don't think so," Michael said. "He has gone on and on about you and me—about our relationship and how we are a better example of marriage than his straight friends. He knows we made our commitment when we thought you had little time left. We took a chance on each other, knowing it could all end tragically. That had a profound effect on him."

"I suppose that would affect anyone with a heart," Scott conceded. "You've always trusted your gut. If you believe his intentions are pure, I can't question that."

"Look, he's a politician. They can't help but look out for themselves. But somehow, this seems different," Michael said. "I believe him."

•••

Michael was organizing the staff in the mayor's office. Before getting his team in place, he was tasked with writing a plan for LGBT folks to marry. He and his staff crafted a simple document stating that

the City of San Francisco recognized marriage between same-sex couples and came up with a simple script for a ceremony. They were on their way. Just over a month into his term as mayor, Gavin Newsom and the City of San Francisco began to issue marriage licenses to same-sex couples. It started quietly, but word spread quickly, and soon there were lines of couples snaking around city hall. As the news got out, the media's attention was almost unbearable. Numerous city officials were deputized to perform weddings throughout the building. They feared that the state could shut them down at any moment. Before it all ended, over four thousand couples were married.

Couples who had been together for ten, twenty, and thirty years and never dreamed of a legal wedding flocked to city hall. Florists gave out free bouquets to couples standing in line, and crowds gathered to cheer on the newlyweds. There were protesters as well, but nothing could quash the excitement. San Francisco was making history.

By the end of the first day, Michael flopped down on a chair in the mayor's office. They were completely wiped out. Newsom looked over at him. "What about you and Scott?"

"It was such a hectic day; I didn't even have time to call him," he responded.

"Call him now," the mayor said, handing Michael the phone. "Tell him to get his butt over here. It's time to get married."

Michael looked at him in disbelief and dialed. When Scott answered, he simply said, "This is the mayor's office. His honor is requesting your presence immediately. And wear a jacket and tie."

Thirty minutes later, long after city hall had closed for the day, an exhausted gaggle of staffers and city officials gathered at the top of the grand staircase of the main entrance. Mayor Newsom stood between Scott and Michael, and for the second time, they pledged their lives to each other. However, this time, it was officially recognized by the City of San Francisco.

"By the powers vested in me by the City of San Francisco, I declare you spouses for life."

With tears in their eyes, they kissed. Then Newsom threw his arms around them, and everyone cheered. It would be an entire month

before the State of California stopped them from issuing licenses. By August, all those marriages would be nullified. But that history-making act of defiance sparked lawsuits claiming that denying marriage to same-sex couples was unconstitutional discrimination. It took four more years, but in 2008, the California Supreme Court legalized same-sex marriage. But it was not to be. An anti-gay marriage proposition was voted in. It was years before the federal courts would overturn it. Nevertheless, the momentum moved in the right direction.

They say the third time's a charm. In 2015, when marriage equality became the law of the land, Scott and Michael got married again. Ideally, they'd use their original wedding date, which would mean waiting for nine months. Scott reluctantly agreed to have yet another wedding ceremony—as long as it wasn't a huge affair. As usual, Michael got his way. Once again, he planned a lavish party with friends and family to mark the legal recognition of their marriage. The struggle took many years, but in the end, they won the battle. There was no question that a celebration was in order.

After so many years together, writing their vows proved to be easier than they thought. Delivering them, however, was not. So many years of pain and struggle, fear and hope, were woven into their words. With eyes that had experienced pain, disease, and death, Scott and Michael penned their thoughts. They were well aware that they had made it through the storm. Declaring their love before friends and family for the third time, the miracle of that love shone brightly that day. Just as he did at their first ceremony, Scott took Michael's hand and shared his heart.

"Michael, we have within us the potential for unconditional and everlasting love. Our life's work is to realize this gift. With our love and encouragement, I will continue to search within myself for these gifts so that I may become whole, to love as generously as you love.

"The hopes and dreams of our young adulthood have been enriched with many experiences, shared friends, great love, fears, grief, and opportunities for growth. Your companionship has given me immeasurable wealth.

"Today, I stand before you, understanding our commitment more fully, changed by our experiences, humbled by the challenges that

I did not meet, and bolstered by the dreams we share.

"I take your hand once again with renewed joy.

"I recommit myself to walking with you.

"I love you in all that is good.

"I love you in all that is challenging.

"I give you my fidelity.

"I will love you in joy and in sorrow and with all that is within me."

Bursting with emotion, Michael fought back his tears and spoke from his soul.

"Scott, As we look at many years of our lives together,

"We know endurance and perseverance.

"We know joy and success,

"Risk and failure.

"In the tumult of that perfect storm, in the blink of an eye, I could have lost you.

"In your determination to embrace life,

"I found in you a man stronger in the face of peril,

"And in myself, a tenderness and an unwavering will to be your champion,

"A force fiercer than I could have imagined.

"In our own way, we have found joy in life's adventures,

"And because we weathered the storm together, we are more sound in our love, more secure in our commitment.

"As we look to the future, I know that my life is more complete because you are by my side.

"I commit to you, once again, my spirit, my heart, and my life."

\#

Decades after they first promised their love, the United States Government legally recognized what was always there. They didn't expect to feel any different, but they did. Somehow, not having to explain their relationship made a difference. Everyone understood what marriage meant. They no longer called themselves partners or lovers. They were husbands.

Tilting Toward the Sun　229

CHAPTER FORTY-TWO
TWENTY-FIVE YEARS
2018

How do you mark twenty-five years of marriage when you never expected to live past the first two? Thinking back, Scott could hardly believe he was still here. At some point, he stopped living as if he were about to die. Rather than trying to fit everything into the little time he had left, he let himself plan for the future.

Scott dared to dream of growing old with Michael, mainly because they were approaching sixty. Certainly not old, but well past his expectations. Scott was excited at the prospect of retiring in Sonoma County. When Michael had mentioned it so many years before, Scott believed it was a fantasy—he would never live that long. Now, the dream of getting a tiny cottage close to a vineyard seemed possible. Perhaps he'd even work part-time doing wine tastings for tourists. Dreaming about their future made him take stock of his past. He could never have imagined all that had come to pass. Ushering so many friends through their battle with AIDS left an indelible mark on his heart. He would always carry those beautiful souls within him. Finding Michael the second time around had transformed his life. It was Michael who gave him the will to fight, to live, to thrive.

Gathered at a bed-and-breakfast in Healdsburg, California, an intimate crew of friends looked forward to a weekend of wine tasting and good food. Michael loved Sonoma County—it was sunny with beautiful hills and a pretty lake. When tired of the foggy San Francisco summers, Scott and Michael stole away to Sonoma, chasing the sunshine and warmth. Over the years, they had witnessed many changes in the quaint villages as they transitioned from one-horse towns to elegant tourist destinations. Once free of charge, wine tastings with guests standing at the counter morphed into costly private events orchestrated by a sommelier who explained the nuances of each grape. Michael and Scott traveled further north to capture the small-town feeling of their first years together in California. Even so, they loved Sonoma and escaped the city fog whenever possible.

Michael had always planned their vacations and social calendar, and Scott was grateful for his boundless energy. Amazed by his ability to bring varied groups of people together, Scott often sat back and marveled at Michael's joyful orchestration of their gatherings. He savored the preparation of scrumptious appetizers and innovative menus. He often selected a theme for their dinners, with music and decorations to accentuate the festivity. Choreographing events was in Michael's wheelhouse. However, for their twenty-fifth-anniversary celebration, Scott took over.

"Please let me organize our anniversary party, Michael," Scott pleaded.

"You? Seriously? You hate making all the plans and attending to details," Michael replied.

"I do, but the burden always falls on you. This time, I want you to sit back and relax. Let me surprise you."

"Yikes," Michael exclaimed. "I'm not sure I'm ready for this. Are you sure you don't want me to help?"

"I've got this. The question is, Mr. Control Freak, can you let go and leave it to me?" Scott asked.

"I'm not sure that's possible. But I promise to try."

Scott found a lovely bed-and-breakfast right on the Russian River in Healdsburg. He planned to fill the entire place with their friends. The

River Belle Inn was still undergoing renovations when Scott contacted them. The manager was thrilled to have a weekend fully booked before they had officially opened. Then he set about inviting friends from city hall, the hospital, and close neighbors and friends. He asked them to keep all the details a secret from Michael. All he said was that they were heading to Sonoma for a romantic getaway.

Leaving San Francisco on a Friday afternoon presented challenges. Traffic on the Golden Gate and Bay Bridges was always heavy. Scott and Michael packed up the car and headed north around 6:00 p.m. Their friends had gotten an earlier start and were waiting for their arrival. Pulling into the driveway of the River Belle, Michael whistled his approval.

"Well done, Dr. Scott! This is beautiful."

"I thought you'd approve. Let's leave the bags in the car for now. I want to show you the view of the river."

Scott took Michael's hand and led him to the backyard. Strings of lights colored the lawn and reflected off the river. The fire pit was aglow, and symphonic music floated through the air.

"Follow me. It's difficult in this light, but you must see the river."

One by one, their friends quietly filled the patio behind them. When Michael turned, they raised their glasses and shouted, "Congratulations!" Michael's face was immobile, and not a sound came from his lips.

"Happy Anniversary, my love," Scott whispered in his ear, and he kissed him on his temple. It was a miracle that his surprise had worked. Michael had a way of sniffing out the details of every event—not this time. He'd rarely seen Michael at a loss for words. The laughter echoed down the river, and the aroma of brick-oven pizza filled the air. Michael looked around at their friends: Kenneth and Lourdes from city hall, Duncan and Jeff, and Scott's old navy pal, Glen, who was there with his date. It was like seeing their shared history gathered in one romantic place. There was nothing fancy about the evening—no china or crystal, no distinguished guests to entertain—just their closest friends, snacks, and superb wine.

"Glen, it's been forever!" Michael exclaimed.

"Too long, my friend. Congratulations," he replied, lifting Michael into a bear hug. Michael squealed with delight.

"And who is this handsome devil by your side?" Michael asked.

"This is Dex. I believe you guys met a few years back."

"And you're still together?" Scott asked as he punched Glen's shoulder.

"Who knew you'd finally settle down?" Michael said.

"I basically had to tie him down," Dex added.

"Hey, now, let's not tell them about all our fetishes," Glen joked. "Seriously, who would have thought that career navy guys could be boyfriends?"

"When are you guys getting married?" Michael asked.

"Dude, one step at a time. We've only been together for five years."

Michael looped his arm into Glen's and whispered, "Time to put a ring on it, sailor!"

Laughter filled the air as Scott and Michael made the rounds, chatting with their friends. Scott wandered over to the river's edge, intoxicated by the sights and sounds around him. He looked back at Michael working the crowd. His silky brown hair had thinned, but his eyes were just as deep. He's more handsome now than ever, he thought. Images of the past floated through his mind. Scott couldn't help but remember all those friends who were missing—Ted, Brian, Roland, and so many others. Roland would have been the life of the party, holding court and playfully critiquing everyone's outfits and cutting them to pieces. Scott smiled despite the ache in his heart. Startling him from his thoughts, Michael slipped his arm around him.

"I know that look. What's on your mind, my love?" Michael asked.

"Oh, just thinking. Roland would have loved this."

"Ted, too." He paused, placing his hand on Scott's heart. "They're still with us, you know. Right here, always."

"We've been through so much together, haven't we?"

"There's still more to come," Michael said.

"This may sound hokey, but there were so many times when it

seemed we were flying too close to the sun. We could have so easily been burned. Standing here with you after twenty-five years together really is a miracle."

"You're right, Scott. Since the day we met, I have been warmed by your love. I've basked in your light and energy. Maybe we didn't fly too close. Maybe we were tilting toward the sun—just enough to be nourished by it, letting it draw us together and help us grow."

Michael leaned up and gently kissed him.

"All right, you two, enough of that!" Glen called out. "You have guests to entertain!"

The wine flowed freely, and the warmth of those gathered filled them with joy. Each had changed their lives, etching their faces in their hearts. They had become part of their story, their history. It was the perfect beginning of their anniversary weekend.

The following morning, the staff served breakfast at tables overlooking the river. People rose at their leisure and filled their bellies with French toast, pancakes, omelets, and crispy bacon. Several minivans pulled up before noon and whisked them away to Jordan Winery for an elegant food and wine-pairing lunch. Several hours passed as they lingered at their tables. Afterward, the crew headed into Healdsburg to walk off their meal in the town square. A local musician sat on a stool under the gazebo and strummed his guitar, singing oldies and encouraging the crowd to join in. Scott took Michael by the hand and wandered into boutique shops lining the square. Michael, never one for window shopping, couldn't resist purchasing several new outfits. Rather than follow his usual script, Scott encouraged him to buy whatever he wanted.

"Is something wrong?" Michael asked. "Am I dying?"

"What do you mean?"

"Come on, Scott. You're usually looking over my shoulder, asking me if I really need a new shirt or tie or whatever. You're being too nice."

"Enjoy it while it lasts. Next week, it's back to normal."

•••

The following day, after checking out, they all met in town for lunch. The celebration continued with good food and silly stories. When

the check came, Michael was sorry to see it end.

"Before you guys go, let's take a selfie!"

"Great idea, Michael," said Glen. "Let me take it, and I can AirDrop it to everyone."

They gathered around with the redwoods of the Healdsburg town center looming behind them. Just as the photo was being taken, Glen gave them instructions.

"Everyone say: 'QUEEN!'"

Pealing with laughter, the crew shouted. Passersby laughed along with the jovial party and applauded. And just like that, it was over. Bidding goodbye to each of their friends, Michael's heart was full. Even after all these years together, Scott continued to amaze him. He had planned every detail of a beautiful anniversary weekend. It couldn't have been more perfect. Climbing into the car, he leaned over to kiss his husband.

"You are the most wonderful man. You know that? In fact, you're my favorite husband."

"So, I've surpassed all the others?"

"Yes, by far. First of all, you exist, whereas the others..."

"That's quite a high bar you've set for me," Scott said, shaking his head.

"Seriously. Thank you. This has been the best gift you could have given me for our anniversary."

"It's not over yet, my dear. We have one more appointment this afternoon."

"Please, no more wine tasting. I don't think I can drink another drop."

"No more wine. There's something I want you to see."

Keeping the details to himself, Scott drove onto Highway 101 and headed north. Michael chatted animatedly for the entire drive. He loved reliving each moment of their special occasions, so he recounted his every thought from the moment they arrived in Healdsburg on Friday night. The image of the Russian River dotted with lights on their first evening remained with him. The gathering of friends colored the already evocative scene with deeper meaning. These people had journeyed with

them through trials and triumphs. Throughout their lives together, they had been blessed with a chosen family. And they would always be there for them. Michael mentioned each by name as he recalled that first night. He was taking stock of their lives and what mattered most.

Michael barely noticed Scott exiting the freeway, heading for the Citrus Fair. At a stoplight, he finally asked. "What is this, Scott? It looks like a vast parking lot. Where are we?"

"This is Cloverdale. Before the vineyards took over, Sonoma County was home to groves of citrus and prune trees. They were the predominant crops, and every year since the late 1800s, the harvest has been celebrated with a huge festival. The fairgrounds are also home to the largest wine competition in North America. There's a lot of history here."

"I've never even heard of Cloverdale. I think the furthest north we've ever traveled was Healdsburg," Michael replied.

"Yeah, I did some research when planning our anniversary, and this town sounded intriguing."

"It's so quaint. Can we get out and walk a bit?"

It was an exceptionally sleepy Sunday afternoon. They parked near the town square and wandered the neighborhood. They stopped in a coffee shop called The Plank, where the barista greeted them as invited guests.

"Good afternoon, fellas. What brings you to our little hamlet?"

"My husband and I spent the weekend in Healdsburg celebrating our twenty-fifth anniversary. We've never been this far north, so we're exploring the area," Michael responded.

"Congratulations! Then, these are on the house," the barista said, handing over their lattes.

"Just curious about the stage across the street. What is that used for?" Scott asked.

"Ah, that's the scene of Cloverdale's famous Friday Night Live. It's a great community event for our town. We have live music and food every Friday throughout the summer. Bands from all over come and perform, and everyone turns out for it."

"How cool is that? We have to come back for that, Scott."

"You won't be disappointed," the barista replied. "It's so much fun."

They resumed their walk, commenting on the cute houses in the downtown neighborhood. Once again, Michael fantasized about retiring in Sonoma.

"Wouldn't it be fabulous to live up here, Scott? Wandering through vineyards, going to wine tastings."

A block or two away from the main square, a "For Sale" sign hung outside a quaint cottage. Scott ambled up the path to the front door.

"Do you think they'll let us in?" he asked mischievously.

"Come on, Scott. That's not right. You can't disturb them. Let's go."

Ignoring Michael's protests, Scott rang the bell. When the door opened, a young man greeted him with a radiant smile.

"You must be Scott. I'm Chad. Come on in."

Confused, Michael's jaw dropped as he followed Scott into the house. Room by room, Chad described special features and what had been renovated. Then, he gave them a more extensive history of Cloverdale while Scott peppered him with questions.

"OK, I'll leave you boys alone to chat," Chad said. "If you have any more questions, I'll be in the kitchen."

As soon as he disappeared from their sight, Michael gave Scott a look.

"What are you up to, Scott?"

"Don't you just love this place?"

"I do. It's adorable. But why are we here?"

"We've always dreamed of having a place here in Sonoma. The more I learned about Cloverdale, the more I liked it. What do you think? Would this place fit the bill?"

"Oh, my God. You're serious."

"I am, Michael. If there is one thing we've learned, it's that life is short. If we don't take advantage of what life presents, it may never be offered again. Our first years were filled with such uncertainty. The fact that I didn't become another statistic was a bona fide miracle. Neither of

us believed we'd celebrate five years together, let alone twenty-five. But here we are. Let's make sure we celebrate life at every turn. It's you who made me want to live, you who gave me the strength to fight—you who gives meaning to my life. So, what do you say? Shall we begin the next stage of our journey together? Shall we live in wine country?"

"Scott, my life with you has been one unexpected grace after another. How could I possibly refuse an offer like that?"

As if on cue, a cork popped, and Chad appeared with champagne. Scott raised his glass and gazed into Michael's eyes.

"Here's to another twenty-five years with the love of my life!"

THE END

Dr. Mario Dell'Olio is a 2022 winner of the Premio Vincenzo Crocitti International award for literature and music. He is the author of several books: Letters from Italy is the love story of his immigrant parents. A memoir, Coming About: Life in the Balance, is about a sailing adventure going terribly wrong. Body And Soul, is an LGBTQA+ fiction that explores the strife of coming out during the 1980s. New Men: Bonds of Brotherhood, is a romantic journey of self-discovery inspired by true stories. Filled with drama, romance, intrigue, corruption, & the search for meaning. Forbidden Rome is a re-telling of New Men.

He is the music director at an independent school in Sonoma County, California. Previously, he was chair of the music department and ethics teacher at a school for girls in Manhattan. Dr. Mario Dell'Olio conducted the Concert and Chamber Choirs. He has led his choirs on international and domestic concert tours and released numerous albums on iTunes and Amazon.com. Dr. Dell'Olio was director of music at

Mission Dolores Basilica in San Francisco, California, from 1990 to 2000. He led the Basilica Choir's first international concert tour to Italy in June 1999. Dr. Dell'Olio holds a Doctor of Sacred Music, a Master of Music in Vocal Performance, and a Master of Religious Education. He pursued postgraduate work in Theology at the Pontifical Gregorian University, Rome, Italy.

With over 36,000 followers on Twitter and a solid social media presence, he actively participates in the Writing Community. Dr. Dell'Olio has scheduled numerous author events, readings, and book signings. In November 2020, The Empire City Men's Chorus of New York City performed a concert/documentary based on Dell'Olio's book, Coming About.

https://mariodellolio.com

NOTE FROM THE AUTHOR

Word-of-mouth is crucial for any author to succeed. If you enjoyed Tilting Toward the Sun, please leave a review online—anywhere you are able. Even if it's just a sentence or two. It would make all the difference and would be very much appreciated.

Thank You!

Mario Dell'Olio

www.ingramcontent.com/pod-product-compliance
Lightning Source LLC
Chambersburg PA
CBHW072153070526
44585CB00015B/1119